MAKERS AND MOLDERS
OF THE RESTORATION MOVEMENT

A STUDY OF LEADING MEN
AMONG THE CHURCH OF CHRIST

BY J.J. HALEY

Charleston, AR:
Cobb Publishing
2020

Makers and Molders of the Restoration Movement: A Study of Leading Men Among the Church of Christ is published in the United States of America by:

Cobb Publishing
704 E. Main St.
Charleston, AR 72933
www.CobbPublishing.com
CobbPublishing@gmail.com
479.747.8372

ISBN: 978-1-947622-45-6

PUBLISHER'S PREFACE

The book you hold in your hands (or are reading on a screen) is—let's not sugarcoat it—somewhat biased. But, we believe that it does hold value because of the history it records, and the succinctness in which it does it. Let's face it, most people aren't going to read an entire book dedicated to any of the individuals presented here, so this book can help give you a good overview of their lives and work in a relatively short period of time and pages.

J.J. Haley was not what you'd call a "conservative" among those connected with the Restoration Movement. He generally aligned himself with the more liberal element (using instruments, supporting the missionary society, endorsing evolution, etc.), which becomes evident when you read portions of this work.

We have taken the liberty of tweaking the original title (*Makers and Molders of the **Reformation** Movement*) to better reflect the actual contents, and to not confuse readers who might be expecting to read about men like Martin Luther, John Calvin, and Ulrich Zwingli.

Other than a handful of instances where we have changed the word "Reformation" to "Restoration" (again, to better reflect the content), the text of the book remains as it did in its original edition.

May you find the information interesting, and the examples of dedication to the Word of God encouraging!

Bradley S. Cobb
Publisher

CONTENTS

THOMAS CAMPBELL 1
*Creative Personality of the
Union Movement of the Nineteenth Century* 1

ALEXANDER CAMPBELL 11
Prophet and Leader of the Restoration Movement 11

BARTON W. STONE 23
*Prophet of Evangelism and Piety
in the Restoration Movement* 23

WALTER SCOTT 33
Masterful Preacher and Teacher 33

ISAAC ERRETT 45
Major Prophet of the Second Generation of Disciples 45

MOSES E. LARD 57
*Prophet of Radicalism, Literalism, and Conservatism in the
Second Generation of the Restoration Movement* 57

**WINTHROP H. HOPSON
AND GEORGE W. LONGAN** 71
*Two Representative Types of Leadership
in the Middle Period of Our History* 71

**JOHN W. MCGARVEY
AND ALEXANDER PROCTER** 85
*Two Representatives of Conservative
and Progressive Leadership* 85

THE RESTORATION MOVEMENT UP TO DATE
.... 101

THOMAS CAMPBELL

Creative Personality of the Union Movement of the Nineteenth Century

WHEN a religion comes into the world with vitality enough to survive in the struggle for existence, four things happen in the working out of its problems.

First, a supreme creative personality appears, who, passing the truth through the alembic[1] of his genius, molds it into a vital and consistent whole. A second personality, one or more, but little inferior to the first, comes after the founder, a man of interpretative genius, who interprets and mediates the truth in the application of its principles to life. Creation and interpretation call for a third man or men in the supreme order, call for a man of constructive ability, architectonic power, a builder who organizes the religion into a system and the church into methods, forms, and an order of administration. It is in this period of organization that the ecclesiastic, the priest and creed maker get in their oars. Inspiration is succeeded by convention, the spirit by the letter, and things drop to a lower level. The lofty ideals of the founder and his first interpreters are blurred, confused and lost. Corruption and stagnation come in like a flood. This is the reformer's opportunity, and reformation, necessitated by conditions, runs along historic lines similar to those of the original faith itself.

Moses was the creative personality of Judaism, the great prophets were his interpreters. Ezra and Nehemiah organized the law into Leviticism. During the exile and after the restoration, the Divine Legation of Moses was organized into later Judaism, an inferior product of ecclesiasticism and priestcraft. Dead consciences, lowered moral standards, corruption in faith and life, formalism, hypocrisy and shallowness; no open vision, no inspired

---

[1] Distilling apparatus.—Editor.

prophet to correct abuses till John the Reformer appears in the wilderness, calling upon the people to hark back to the founder and his first interpreters. "Prepare ye the way of the Lord, make his paths straight."

Four Periods of Religious History

Jesus of Nazareth was the creative personality of Christianity, John and Paul were his first great interpreters, the Greek period organized theology and the Roman period organized the church. Organization was the straight way to crystallization, life and passion went out, corruption and tradition came in. Theological degradation, ecclesiastical prostitution, creed making, sect building, low grade morals in the life of the church, and the dark ages came on for a thousand years. Prophet reformers arose who felt the darkness and saw the light: Savonarola in Italy, Huss in Bohemia, Tyndall in England, Layfevre in France, Luther in Germany. The dawn was breaking, and when Luther nailed his theses to the door of the university church at Wittenburg, the Reformation Ship was launched, the banner of Apostolic Christianity was flung to the breeze.

The four periods, therefore, through which the evolution of the Christian religion has passed have been the creative, the interpretative, the constructive, and the reformative— creation, interpretation, construction and reformation. Reform and restoration movements pass through similar phases. St. Augustine was the creative, originating personality of Calvinism, John Calvin and Jonathan Edwards were its great interpreters, John Knox was the organizing genius of the Calvinistic reformation.

The Creative Personality of Our Movement

Thomas Campbell, author of the Declaration and Address, and founder of the Christian Association of Washington, Pa., was the creative personality of our restoration movement. Alexander, his son, and Isaac Errett of the second generation of Disciples, were his great interpreters. We are now, and have been for thirty years, in the throes of the constructive and organizing era of our reformatory experience. In the absence of conspicuous personal leadership in this branch of the service, our organizing genius has yet to appear. Most of our troubles have arisen, and are likely to continue to arise, as in other reforming movements. As Thomas Campbell was the Moses of our Restoration, the Declaration and Address was the Deuteronomy of our prophetic reformation. As certainly as the fifth book of Moses contains the basic principles and the whole body of teaching and ideals of the prophets that inspired and entered into the structure of the Deuteronomic reformation in Israel, this matchless document, whose origin we celebrated four years ago, embraces every truth we have taught, every principle we have advocated, every ideal we have striven to realize in the hundred years of our existence.

The Declaration and Address

Father Campbell was the originator. The illustrious son was the advocate, the expounder, the defender, the illuminator, the adaptor of the teaching of his father in the constitution of the Christian Association, the Sermon on the Mount of our New Testament, if you will allow me to change the figure from a discourse of Moses in the Old Testament to a discourse of Christ in the New. The relation of the Sermon on the Mount to the kingdom of God is the relation of the Declaration and Address to our religious reformation. The effort that has been made to trace the Christian unity conception and emphasis to Thomas Campbell, and the primitive Christianity idea as the basis of union, to Alexander Campbell, and to make the two stand over against each other as variant reforming types, has not been a success. The fact is, the two conceptions, as common integers of New Testament Christianity, were emphatically and profusely taught by the elder Campbell in the historic document penned a hundred years ago in Washington, Pa. I have been amazed at the comprehensiveness and all-inclusiveness of this composition. It is the most admirable summary of apostolic Christianity to be found in the literature of the church this side of the New Testament. Even from the point of view of modern criticism, which has claimed so many new discoveries, we are chagrined to find that Father Campbell has stolen all our good ideas. The unification of Christendom on the basis of the apostolic faith in Jesus Christ, the restoration of the church with its divine equipment for human service, "the union of all who love in the service of all who suffer," the purification and elevation of morals to make way for the building of character after the likeness of Christ, opposition to a fake mysticism in conversion, and all divisive and corrupting instruments, such as human creeds and an ignorant ministry; these and all other essential and vital things that pertain to the kingdom of God and the name of Jesus Christ are distinctly and explicitly taught, so that we have preached nothing the last hundred years, and will preach nothing in the oncoming centuries, not advanced, or at least suggested, in this magna charta of our restoration movement.

European Sources of Restoration Movement

I am not saying these things, of course, in ignorance of the fact that many of the root principles of the restoration can be traced to European soil. Both of the Campbells were of European birth and education, and there was much in religious training and social environment to suggest the need of reformation, and a cue to their future work. When Thomas Campbell set sail for the United States, in 1807, a revolt against Calvinism, and hairbrained mysticism had gained a foothold in Scotland. More than one harbinger had arisen in the wilderness of sectarianism to restore the tabernacle of the Lord that had fallen down. John Glass and his son-in-law, Sandeman; the Haldane Brothers, and Greville Ewell, of Glasgow, were striking powerful blows at Calvinistic theology, the corrupt condition of religious society, and the divided state of the church. Successive attempts at reformation since Luther had culminated in a new effort, at the beginning of the nineteenth century, to get back to Christ and the apostles. These efforts, however, were tentative and partial, and short-lived for lack of genius and personality in leadership. They were quite successful in their diagnosis of the situation, which called aloud for the restoration of the ancient order of things, and the remedies suggested were adequate to meet the needs of the case, the moment was imminent, but the man did not appear. He had emigrated to the United States. The field of a great apostolic restoration movement had been transferred from Scotland to North America; from the Old World to the New.

People not acquainted with the subject are surprised to find in the books of Glass and Sandeman, the Haldanes and Dr. Kirk, ideas, arguments, doctrines, and even phrases, that our reformation has made familiar to the world. These men did not fail to grasp the truth, and to realize the contrast between what they saw and what Christ intended; but they lacked the power and the opportunity to incarnate these principles in a personality strong enough in creative and adaptive genius to make the movement go in the face of old world difficulties. It was on this side of the Atlantic that the man and the moment came together.

The Man and the Opportunity

When the Campbells set foot on American soil, they found the situation worse, the circumstances of contending sects calling more loudly for reform, than in the old world. They found more dogmatism, a fiercer sectarianism, a more intense fanaticism, a wilder mysticism, a narrower, harder, and less tractable denominationalism than they had left behind them in Europe. If the people were not hateful, they certainly hated one another. Thomas Campbell tells of a seceder divine who was so intensely human that he exhorted his congregation : "I beseech you, my brethren, to hate all other denominations, especially the Catholics." An age of increasing sects, multiplying creeds, contending parties, and warring zealots, had reached the stage where reaction must begin to rally the forces of reformation. The time had come to knock down the Dagons of theology in the temple of sectarianism, and to call back a divided church from the wilderness of strife and bitterness to the unity of the Spirit in the bond of peace.

The American Church in the Nineteenth Century

Three things had happened to bring about this ecclesiastical reign of terror: First, the Bible had been lost in the church; second, Christ had been lost in the Bible; third, the church had been lost in the world. The first thing a corrupt church does is to lose its Bible, and the Bible is never lost in but one place, and that is in the temple. The first thing a restored church does is to find the Book and put it in the place where it belongs. The greatest spiritual reformation in Israel synchronized with the discovery of the book of Deuteronomy in the Temple, where it had been lost during the reign of corrupt Manasseh. John the Harbinger launched his revolution by a rediscovery of the Book of the Law and the Prophets in the same old place of hiding, the Temple in Jerusalem. In the Reformation of the sixteenth century, Martin Luther found the Holy Scriptures buried in a dead language, and a Standard Bible chained to the lectern of a Holy Catholic Church. The Book had to be liberated from its temple prison, and a translation of it made into the common vernacular before reformation truth could find a place in the consciousness of the people.

Back to the "Book of Books"

The new religious freedom that came in with Luther had its evil side. The abuse of liberty brought in the era of sectarianism and denominationalism. Two hundred years of warring creeds and bellicose denominations, and history repeats itself. The Bible is again lost in a superincumbent mass of ignorance and superstition and pharisaism, and the fate of the Bible is always the fate of Christ and the church. Necessarily, therefore, the first characteristic of our restoration movement was the rediscovery of the Holy Scriptures. The assertion of the authority of the divine Word and its all-sufficiency as a rule of faith and practice was the first step towards realizing the need of reform. "Where the Scriptures speak we speak, and where the Scriptures are silent we are silent." The life and power of every forward movement in the history of organized Christianity is a fresh and vital re-interpretation of the Bible and a new application of its principles to the life of the church. And this, of necessity, leads straight to the rediscovery of Christ, and his installation on the throne of universal empire and Lordship, followed by the restoration of the New Testament church. Mr. Campbell was quick to see that any effective appeal to the conscience of the Christian world must involve a fresh and living interpretation of Holy Scripture, a vital and loyal recognition of Christ as Prophet, Priest, and King, as Savior and Lord of all, and an earnest effort towards the realization of the ideals of the apostolic church, before it was possible for the Savior's intercessory prayer to be answered—"that they all may be one," as He and the Father are one. The plea was for the unity, purity, spirituality, and catholicity of the New Testament church, fresh from the hands of Christ, and guided by the Holy Spirit in the apostles. A careful analysis of the Declaration and Address will show that this plea for unity was simple, scriptural and catholic, an appeal to the conscience of the universal church.

Catholicity of Our Plea

The catholic creed of Christendom, "I believe that Jesus is the Christ, the Son of the living God, the Savior and Lord of Men."
The catholic rule of faith and practice, the Word of God, written in the Old and New Testaments.
The catholic ordinances, baptism and the Lord's Supper.
The catholic name, Christian.
The catholic life, the ethics of the kingdom of God, "Whatsoever

things are true, whatsoever things are honest, whatsoever things are just, whatsoever things are pure, whatsoever things are lovely, of good report, if there be any virture, if there be any praise, think on these things."

This plea is reasonable, feasible, beautiful, and, in time, must become universal. The spiritual movement originated and consecrated in the manner I have endeavored to describe, and brought forth on this new American continent in the last hundred years, is not a reformation of existing institutions in the ordinary sense of that term, nor a restoration of primitive Christianity in the sense of literally restoring the historic apostolic church. It is a realization movement whose aim and purpose is to realize the ideals of New Testament Christianity in the life of these modern centuries. It was found not possible to reform existing religious institutions, nor to restore the primitive church by transferring it literally and bodily to the nineteenth century, but it was possible and eminently desirable to make an honest effort to realize the ideals of the apostolic faith that shine and make their appeal from every page of the inspired record.

The Peculiar Glory of "The Current Reformation"

This feature differentiates the movement inaugurated by Thomas Campbell from all of the mere reformations in the history of the church. The old reformations would need to be repeated through successive generations till the end of time; but what we have chosen to call "the current reformation," if rightly understood, forever remains current, because it embodies a principle that makes crystallization forever impossible and growth forever necessary. So long as we strive to actualize the originals, to realize the ideals of the inspired Christianity of the New Testament, we safeguard our religion from stagnation, open the road to perpetual progress, and thus forestall the necessity of further efforts at reformation. This is the peculiarity and glory of our great religious movement, and if, under

God, we are faithful to the charge committed to our care, we shall contribute our share and more to the bringing in of that far-off divine event to which the whole creation moves, when they shall not teach every man his neighbor, and every man his brother, saying, "Know the Lord, for all shall know him, from the least to the greatest of these."

ALEXANDER CAMPBELL
Prophet and Leader of the Restoration Movement

ALEXANDER CAMPBELL was in the twenty-first year of his age when he joined his distinguished father in Washington, Pa. Thomas Campbell had preceded his family by two years, coming to these shores from the old world in 1807. His family, essaying to follow him a year later, were shipwrecked off the coast of Scotland and were compelled to return to the old country, where they remained a year before again setting sail. This calamity and subsequent detention turned out to be a providence, as far as the future of young Alexander and the reformation he was destined to lead, were concerned. The opportunity which it gave him of three hundred days' study in the University of Glasgow, and association with leaders of religious thought in Scotland, was joyfully embraced, and always in after years acknowledged as potential in its influence on his future life and work.

The previous education of this coming reformer had been in no less efficient hands than that of his eminent father. In the days of his adolescent youth he had shown a marked indisposition to study and all indoor confinement. A stout and vigorous lad, overflowing with animal spirits and in love with God's great out-of-doors, he was fond of fishing, gunning, trapping wild animals, and wandering in the fields of his native heather. Athletic sports had more attraction for him than the serious business of acquiring an education. James Foster, a friend of the family, says the first time he saw Alexander Campbell, a boy of fifteen summers, he had a long pole in his hand with a net attached to one end with which he was catching small birds under the eaves of the houses in the outskirts of the town.

Like Adam Clark in his youthful days, our nascent genius evinced but little ambition for the acquisition of knowledge. He went out under a shade tree one day to croon over his French lesson in "The Adventures of Telemachus." A warm summer day, he was overcome by the spirit of drowsiness, and falling into a deep slumber, a cow came along, seized his Telemachus and actually devoured it. On reporting the disaster at home his father administered a sound thrashing and told him by way of further humiliation, that "the cow had more French in her stomach than he had in his head," a fact too obvious to be easily denied.

This love of sport and the exuberance of animal vitality in the activities of outdoor life, tended to the toughening of fiber and the development of a powerful physique that stood him well in hand in the strenuous responsibilities and labors of after life. It was not long after the Telemachus episode till the physical energy of the boy began to transmute itself into the intellectual aptitudes and powers of the man. John Locke's "Letters on Toleration" and his "Essay on the Human Understanding" were the first books that made a profound and lasting impression on his mind. These books of the English philosopher, in fact, laid the foundation of Mr. Campbell's theology and his conception of religious and civil liberty. The association of father and son with the Rich Hill Independents, who were more liberal and catholic in their sympathies than any of the sects of Scotch Presbyterianism, had much to do with the initial impulse of reform and progress in their minds.

Religious Influences of His Youth

After the shipwreck and the return of the family to Glasgow, Alexander was brought into connection more or less intimate with the Haldane Brothers and their new Baptist denomination. The Haldanes were philanthropists and reformers, pleading for some of the principles that afterwards characterized the reformation of the Campbells. The Haldanean movement in Scotland was the "immersion wing" of Sandemanianism, which terminated in the formation of the Scotch Baptists, from which the Old Disciples in Europe borrowed their ecclesiology, in such practices as mutual edification and close communion. Sandeman himself and his father-in-law, Glass, led the Paedo-baptist wing, but Alexander Campbell never accepted the Sandemanian theology in either of its branches. He sympathized with these reformers in their revolt against Calvinism, in their plea for religious liberty, the rights of conscience, and the restoration of the New Testament interpretation of religion; he differed from them on other points of their contention. He listened with a measure of appreciation to the conversations and sermons of John Walker, the founder of the Plymouth Brethren, but never at any time was he even tinctured with the peculiarities of "Brethrenism."

His Entrance into His Life Task

Providentially, young Campbell, in the susceptible and formative years of his life, was so placed and environed as to breathe the atmosphere of religious revival and theological reform, by way of education and preparation for the great leadership to which God was soon to call him. When God raises a man up to perform a great task, he is prepared for its performance, and the preparatory experience in Scotland was the preliminary stage in the education and inspiration of a prophet-reformer who was soon to take his place as leader of one of the great religious movements of history. The man and the movement were about to coincide, as they always do when the hand of God directs the conjunction. The man was being prepared and the moment was approaching.

When young Campbell reached the United States and joined his father at Washington, Pa., the work of union and restoration had already begun. "The Declaration and Address," the constitution of the Christian Association just organized, was passing through the press. The father submitted the proof sheets to his son, who read them with sympathetic interest and profound approval. He lost no time in expressing his determination to spend his life in the advocacy and dissemination of the principles so ably set forth in that immortal document. The sole object of Thomas Campbell in organizing the society known as the Christian Association of Washington was the inculcation of pure evangelical religion and the promotion of Christian unity. The constructive genius of Alexander Campbell led him not only to clear the ground for the unification of Christendom by the destruction of sectarianism and human creeds that made the separating walls between the churches, but he sought as the most fundamental thing, a basis of union, the foundation of the reconstituted universal church of the Apostolic age. It had been learned by experience and perceived, at a glance, by observation that the viperous intolerance and bigotry of sectarianism, and the tweedledum and tweedledee differences of opinion between warring denominations, were the great hindrances to the unity among his disciples for which the Savior prayed. It was this consideration that led to the war on human creeds and opinionism by the Campbells and their coadjutors. It was perceived that these human formularies stopped growth, hindered progress, made men dishonest, and ministered everywhere to theological crystallization fatal to the unity of the spirit in the bond of peace.

Divine and Man-made Creeds

Beginning, as they did, with the presupposition that the Bible of the Old and New Testaments was the Word of God and the only law of faith and practice among Christians, they reasoned, if a human creed contains more than the Bible it contains too much, if it contains less than the Bible it contains too little; if it contains anything different from the Bible it is wrong; if it contains nothing more and nothing less and nothing different from the Bible, it is not a human creed but the Bible itself, the only inspired and all-sufficient rule of faith and morals.

As remarked in the article on Thomas Campbell, all religious reformations in any way related to the history of Christianity, begin, not with the discovery of a new Bible, but the re-discovery of the old one. All progressive and really effective movements within the sphere of the Christian faith must begin with a fresh and vital interpretation of holy Scripture. It was the consciousness of this fact that led Alexander Campbell at the beginning to honestly and fearlessly re-examine his religious position in the light of the inspired teaching of Christ and the apostles. In line with this conviction and while pursuing a de novo investigation of his Greek New Testament, the fact, in the face of all his prejudices, and pre-conceived opinions, dawned upon him that immersion was the form of baptism commanded by Christ and practiced by his first disciples.

Magnificent Loyalty to the Word of God

It has been impossible from the first for any man to rightly understand or properly appraise the reformation inaugurated by the Campbells without taking into account their magnificent loyalty to the Word of God, and its relation to these men and their teaching. The now familiar utterance of the Declaration and Address, "Where the Bible speaks, we speak, and where the Bible is silent we are silent," provoked the remark from Alexander to his father. "If you carry that out it will put an end to infant baptism." The inspired Word is the source of religious knowledge, the channel of divine authority, and the means of spiritual edification, and because infant baptism is not taught therein, it must not be practiced or tolerated in the church of Jesus Christ. The immersion of penitent believers into the name of the Father, the Son, and the Holy Spirit, for the remission of sins, is plainly taught in the Scriptures, therefore the Campbells were immersed, and all who followed them into the union movement of the current reformation. Nothing is to enter into the program of preaching and practice not definitely authorized by the Word of God, in positive command, necessary inference, or approved example. On these ancient Scriptures, inspired by the Holy Ghost, Jesus of Nazareth is enthroned as divine Savior and Lord of all, the foundation of the church, the object of Christian faith, and the inspiration of Christian character.

The Substance of Mr. Campbell's Plea

The scattered and warring fragments of Christendom can only be gathered together on the basis of one Lord, one faith, one baptism, one body, one spirit, one hope of the divine calling, declared by the apostle Paul in his letter to the Ephesians. The existing church could not be reconstructed out of the old material of human opinions and dogmatic speculations, but the New Testament message and order of life could be restored by an honest effort to realize apostolic ideals in the life of today.

This in substance was Mr. Campbell's plea for the ancient gospel and the restoration of the Word to its rightful place as teacher of God and righteousness, the personality of Jesus Christ which the Bible records, and discloses the way, the truth, and the life, the unchanged and unchangeable basis of unity among the people of God, which unity was necessary to the conversion of the world, and the coming in of the kingdom.

Making the Word Clear and Simple

The new quest for truth and righteousness on the pages of that Divine Library, known as ha Biblos (The Book), naturally led the Campbells to stress the importance of the application of sane, practical, and common-sense rules of interpretation to the sacred writings, written under circumstances so different from the ones under which we now live. The canons of historical and literary criticism made familiar by recent Biblical studies were thought out and used by this illuminating interpreter of the Holy Scriptures. No interpretation of the Bible has come to us more intelligent and intelligible, more perspicacious and luminous, more stimulating and suggestive than that which bears the imprimatur of the genius of Alexander Campbell. "Intellectuals" and the best informed among his contemporaries expressed their amazement at the flood of light thrown by his writings and sermons on the pages of God's Bible.

A Sermon that Told

Raccoon John Smith, a born wit and man of genius, who became a mighty preacher of the ancient gospel, tells of the first sermon he heard Alexander Campbell preach:

"He commenced in the usual way, and read the allegory of Sarah and Hagar in the fourth chapter of Galatians. After a general outline of the whole epistle, and how it ought to be read, in order to a correct understanding of the apostle's meaning, he commenced directly on the allegory. I watched all the time with my whole mind to find out to what 'ism' he belonged, but he seemed to move in a higher sphere than that in which these 'isms' abounded. In a simple, plain and artless manner, leaning with one hand on the head of his cane, he went through his discourse. No gesture or any kind of mannerism characterized him, or served to call off the mind from what was being said.

"The congregation being dismissed, I said to Brother Vaughan, 'Is it not a little hard to ride thirty miles to hear a man preach thirty minutes?'

"'Oh,' said he, 'he has been longer than that. Look at your watch.'

"On looking, I found it had been two hours and thirty minutes, and simply said, 'Two hours of my time are gone and I know not how, though wide-awake.'

"Returning to Brother Reynolds, Brother Vaughan asked me, 'Did you find out whether he was a Calvinist or an Arminian?'

"'No, I know nothing about him, but, be he devil or saint, he has thrown more light on that epistle and the whole Scriptures than I have heard in all the sermons I ever listened to before.'"

Dr. Richardson, in his Memoirs of Alexander Campbell, said of T.M. Allen, an eminent preacher who came into the reformation from the Stone movement in Kentucky:

> "He had obtained the '*Christian Baptist*' soon after it commenced, and was delighted with its development of the simple nature of the religion of Christ, its distinctions between dispensations, and the new light which it threw upon the themes of the Bible. He quickly abandoned all the speculations for which, with others, he had been contending, and accustomed himself to speak always of Bible things in Bible words."

Rightly Dividing the Word

Perhaps the most important contribution Mr. Campbell made to Biblical interpretation and theology, was the insistence on dispensational distinctions. With great clearness and cogency he traced the evolution of religion through its well-marked stages which he characterized as the starlight, moonlight, and sunlight dispensations of revelation, running from Adam through the Patriarchs, prophets, and the Jewish economies, to its culmination in Christ, the Light of the World. These distinctions enabled him to make a rational and practical division and application of the Word.

The prophets, priests and sages of the Old Testament prepare us for the advent of the world's Redeemer; the four historic memorials, Matthew, Mark, Luke and John, were written to convince mankind that Jesus of Nazareth was the Messiah, the Christ, the Son of God; the Acts of the Apostles indicted as records of the ministry of the Holy Spirit through the apostles, the conversion of sinners under the Great Commission, and the organization of Christian churches; the apostolic epistles were sent out as manuals of instruction on how to live the Christian life; the apocalypse of St. John, the last book in the canon of Holy Scripture, communicated to the churches a prophetic vision of the struggles of the Kingdom against paganism and its final triumph over the powers of darkness, when the will of God will be done on earth as it is in heaven. The Gospels tell us what to believe in order to become Christians; the Acts of Apostles what to do; the epistles what to be; Revelations what to hope for in the far-off divine event to which the whole creation moves.

By thus rightly dividing the Word of Truth men were saved from the ignorant folly of searching in Ecclesiastes and the Song of Songs for the message of salvation through Jesus Christ, or ransacking Leviticus and Numbers to find an answer to the question: "What must I do to be saved?"

Reaction against Mysticism

In the violent reaction against mysticism and emotional sectarianism, Alexander Campbell, especially in the early day of his reform experiences, went a little too far in the direction of legalism. This was inevitable and to a degree wholesome. Historically considered, there were two Alexander Campbells as distinct in individuality as two different persons. There was the aggressively radical Alexander Campbell No. 1 of the *Christian Baptist* and the Third Epistle of Peter; and the more catholic and spiritual Alexander Campbell No. 2 of the *Millennial Harbinger* and the Lunenburg letter. The early radicalism and legalism of the reformer was the dogmatic and polemic era of the Restoration movement. Both of the Campbells started out in the firm belief that religious controversy was inimical to spirituality and a thing not to be participated in or encouraged. It was an age of theological warfare, polemic strife, a time of what the old colored man called "spute," and the well-meant resolution of abstention from public discussion had to be changed. In self-defense and in vindication of truth and justice, the armor had to be put on, and Mr. Campbell put it on with tremendous effect. His argumentative power and dialectic skill astonished all who heard him in debate.

Rare Argumentative Power

The story told by Bishop Jeremiah Vardeman, a distinguished Baptist minister, who had been chosen as Mr. Campbell's moderator in the debate with McCalla, illustrates Mr. Campbell's renown as a disputant before any of his great debates had been held. Mr. Vardeman, on his way to attend the debate at Washington, Ky., overtook a man on foot. He accosted the stranger and, in good old Kentucky style, asked him where he was going. The man answered that he was on the way to Washington to attend the debate to commence there on the 15th of the month. Taking this traveler on the ankle-bone express to be a zealous Baptist, Vardeman affected to be on the other side, and said, "Is not our man likely to whip your man Campbell?" The man gave him a searching look and asked: "Can you tell me if this is the same Mr. Campbell who debated with Mr. Walker at Mt. Pleasant, Ohio?" Elder Vardeman said he believed he was, to which the stranger replied: "I am not a member of any church. I am going to the debate on the supposition that this is the Mr. Campbell who debated at Mt. Pleasant three years ago. I heard that debate, and all I have to say is, that all creation cannot whip that Mr. Campbell."

The twelve-hour speech in the debate with Robert Owen was a supreme masterpiece of sacred eloquence and argumentation. As an apologetic in defense and vindication of the Christian religion it has never been surpassed in any language. The debates with Presbyterian Rice and Roman Catholic Purcell were monumental triumphs of argumentative genius against the strongest men who could be brought into the field against him. These discussions and frequent preaching excursions into the various states of the Union, together with the publication of many books and his two great periodicals, the *Christian Baptist* and the *Millennial Harbinger*, gave Mr. Campbell ample opportunities for the presentation of his interpretation of Christianity, and very abundant have been the fruits that have followed these efforts. Mr. Campbell's theory of the fundamentals of Apostolic Christianity is his basis for the unification of the broken church, and surely no better basis has ever been suggested, for it is nothing more and nothing less than Jesus Christ as the New Testament interprets him.

BARTON W. STONE

*Prophet of Evangelism and Piety
in the Restoration Movement*

FOUR streams of religious reconstruction broke out almost simultaneously in as many different states of the American Union, springing from a common impulse and motive, but having no organic relation to each other at the beginning.

A Southern Movement

A Methodist minister by the name of James O'Kelly, of North Carolina, after pleading in vain, within the ranks of the Episcopal Methodism, for a congregational system of church government, and the New Testament as the only creed and book of discipline, formally seceded from the Methodist Church in December, 1793.

At first this secession reformation was called "Republican Methodists," but at a conference subsequently held O'Kelly and his followers resolved to be known as Christians only, to acknowledge no head over the church but Christ, and no rule of faith and practice but the New Testament. The spread of this movement has been confined almost entirely to North Carolina and southern Virginia, where churches of this faith and order still exist, and are known as "Christian Churches."

In the New England States

The second stream in the order of time broke out from among the hills of Baptist theology in New England. A physician of Hartland, Vermont, then a member of a Baptist church, became dissatisfied with sectarian names and creeds, began to advocate their abolition, and the substitution of Christian character as the ground of Christian fellowship. In September, 1800, Mr. Jones succeeded in establishing his first church with 25 members, at Lyndon, Vermont. He was joined by several earnest and able preachers, who carried the flaming torch of this unique reformation into several adjoining states. Its uniqueness consisted in the astounding fact that, for the first time since the apostles, churches were being formed on the basis of spiritual character, instead of intellectual creed. Those who were concerned in this movement took the name Christian as their ecclesiastical and personal designation, and adopted the Bible as the only standard of faith and practice.

The Stone Reformation in Kentucky

According to the chronology of events in these historic movements, the Stone reformation comes third, dating its origin from the great revival in 1801 at Caneridge, Bourbon County, Kentucky, eight years earlier than the organization of the Christian Association of Washington, Pa., by Thomas Campbell. In any intelligent investigation of these reformatory origins and influences of the late eighteenth and early nineteenth centuries, the personality and piety of Mr. Stone and his contribution to the religious thought and feeling of the period, are by no means to be overlooked or underestimated.

Barton Stone's Boyhood Environment

Barton Stone was a native of Maryland, born December 24, 1772. He grew to early manhood in Virginia, where he attained great proficiency in his studies, and early mastered all of the ordinary branches of an English education. In 1790 he entered a famous academy in Guilford, North Carolina, for the purpose of obtaining a liberal education, with a view of engaging in the legal profession. Great wars are generally followed by great revivals of religion. After the close of the Revolutionary War, a flame of revival interests swept through the country. Thousands were converted and hundreds of the male converts entered the ministry. The theological war between Methodists and Baptists, the two dominant sects of the South, created perplexity and doubt in the mind of young Stone. He wavered to and fro between the contending parties, till his religious impressions faded, and he settled down in the conviction that there was nothing in religion but occasion for narrowminded people to quarrel.

His Varying Religious Experience

In the meantime, however, a wave of religious enthusiasm struck the town of Guilford; the young man's religious emotions came back, his convictions were deepened, he was converted, made a profession of religion and joined the Presbyterian Church. In his next experience, he was confronted by the problem of entering the ministry. He vacillated here, as he had done before his conversion, in the matter of conflicting opinions of warring sects, not because he was lacking in decision of character, but because of the irrational and repelling theologies delivered from the sacred desks at the time. Calvinism, in all of the naked deformity and monstrosity of the "five points," was the dominant issue. The object of every sermon preached was either to defend Calvinism or to assail it.

Mr. Stone said of that time, "My mind was continually tossed on the waves of speculative divinity, the all-engrossing theme of the religious community at that period. Clashing controversial theories were urged by the different sects with much zeal and bad feeling. There is no surer sign," he declared, "of the low state of true religion." This man of God, long afterwards, delivered his soul and gave expression to his most solemn conviction concerning this abomination of desolation in the Holy Place: "Calvinism is among the heaviest clogs on Christianity in the world. It is a dark mountain between heaven and earth, and is amongst the most discouraging hindrances to sinners from seeking the kingdom of God; and engenders bondage and gloominess in the saints."

He Enters the Presbyterian Ministry

In the titanic struggle with creeds, confessions, and Calvinistic pulpiteers, he was, at least, partially victorious in reaching the conclusion that he had received a call to the ministry of the Presbyterian Church. All of his troubles had not been overcome, for upon application for his ordination papers, he frankly confessed his difficulties to some of the leading ministers of the denomination. These they tried, in vain, to minify or explain away, and finally asked how far he was willing to receive the Confession. He answered, "As far as it is consistent with the Word of God." They concluded this was satisfactory and a sufficient basis on which to proceed with the ordination. Accordingly, when the Presbytery propounded the usual question, "Do you receive and adopt the Confession of Faith, as containing the system of doctrine taught in the Bible?" his public answer was the same as the one he had given in private. However, he was ordained.

The mental reservation with which he accepted the Confession was fatal to orthodox conformity to the Calvinistic standards of Presbyterianism. The more he studied the Confession of Faith the less he liked it. Against its hereditary total depravity, its special grace, particular redemption, miraculous regeneration, unconditional election and reprobation, and damnation generally, his soul revolted with horror and hatred unspeakable. Calvin's God was Stone's Devil.

The Light of the Word Breaks

The psychology of the Stone reformation puts down its finger at this point, and finds the beginning of that revolution in the revulsion of a great soul against the theology of Geneva and the Westminster Divines. Barton W. Stone found his way out of the theological confusions of mystery Babylon as all the reformers before him had done. He is clear and unmistakable on that point. He declares: "From this state of perplexity I was relieved by the precious Word of God. From reading and meditating upon it, I became convinced that God did love the whole world, and that the reason why he did not save all was because of their unbelief, and that the reason why they believed not was not because God did not exert his physical almighty power in them to make them believe, but because they neglected and received not his testimony given in the word concerning his Son, 'These are written that ye might believe that Jesus is the Christ, the Son of God, and that believing ye might have life through his name.'"

It has already appeared in the little that has been said that Barton W. Stone was a man of penetrating mind, benevolent heart, sensitive conscience, fair, broad, and nobly candid, with individuality enough to assert his right to freedom and independence. He had prophetic vision, the power to see truth and to distinguish it from error. There was in him the worst of raw material for the manufacture of a sectarian. He was too large of brain and catholic in spirit to be caught in the toils of a shibboleth-pronouncing religion. His evolution out of the denominational conception of Christianity, and a sectarian interpretation of the Bible, notwithstanding a bad environment, was only a question of time, and not much time at that. The processes of growth, and the bitter opposition that theological growth always excites, did not take long to culminate in ecclesiastical censure and his withdrawal from the Presbyterian Church.

The Great Caneridge Meeting

Shortly before his severance from the Old Connection, he came to the old far-famed bluegrass region of Kentucky, and began to preach, on a wider scale, his new-found gospel of universal love and light. In the month of August, 1801, he began at Caneridge, Bourbon County, what was perhaps the most renowned of the historic revivals in the annals of American evangelization. It was characteristically, and shall we not say, prophetically, a union revival; a number of preachers of "different denominations" taking part in it; but Mr. Stone was the conspicuous personage in preaching and personal leadership. More than 20,000 people came from many counties and from different states, and stayed as long as they could get anything to eat. As noted as Kentuckians are for material supplies and big dinners, this vast concourse of consumers bred a famine in the community. The mighty camp meeting decamped prematurely on account of the exhaustion of food supplies. A tremendous wave of religious excitement and enthusiasm descended upon the great throng as they listened with breathless interest to the word of life. Multitudes of people, many of them infidels and the most hardened sinners, were smitten down like soldiers in battle, and lay motionless for hours, reviving at last to scramble to their feet, either in agonies of remorse or in ecstasies of spiritual joy. These cataleptic convulsions, known at the time as the "jerks" on account of the strange bodily contortions and violent agitations produced, were regarded by Mr. Stone as special manifestations of the power of God in the conversions of men. Perhaps he was right. Any shock, or stroke, or "fit," we should imagine, that would lead unbelievers and case-hardened sinners to a consciousness of their need of repentance and salvation through Jesus Christ, might justly be regarded as the work and power of God.

Ripeness of the Times

The profound and far-reaching significance of this Caneridge revival cannot be adequately appreciated, unless we consider the dark background of infidelity and worldliness then existing in the United States, from which it was the first great reaction. French atheism that followed the Revolution and eighteenth century English Deism, held the field, followed by the recrudescence of a crass paganism in life and morals. The church had become a Kilkenny cattery and had well nigh threshed itself to death on silly dogmatic issues, from one end of the line to the other. James Lane Allen in his "Choir Invisible" is authority for the statement that a batch of 100 copies of "Payne's Age of Reason," sold like hot cakes on the streets of Lexington, Ky., one hundred and fifteen years ago. At that time, and during the incumbency of the great Timothy Dwight at Yale, there were but few students in the college who had the courage to acknowledge themselves Christians and members of churches.

There were numerous infidel societies named after prominent French skeptics of the period. Ministers of that day rode to their appointments with a New Testament in one end of their saddle-bags and a bottle of whiskey in the other, and sometimes they failed to materialize on account of a slight attack of "overstimulation."

The people had grown tired of infidel paganism, both intellectual and practical, and put, therefore, a corresponding energy and earnestness into the evangelical reaction, which had its first great innings at Caneridge. The religious excitement evoked in this meeting did not, like a similar phenomenon in the more recent Welsh revival, react injuriously upon the spiritual life of the people, but continued for many years in the increased faith and fervid devotion of the churches.

It may be said. I think, in perfect historical fairness to all concerned, that the sustained evangelistic enthusiasm and success characteristic of the Disciples during the hundred years of their existence, had one of its chief sources here at Caneridge; although it has never been quite as emotional and perfervid as the type of this early experience. The Disciples brought an intellectual element in that modified it considerably in this particular.

The Movement Spreads

By the time this stage in the evolution of the Stone movement had been reached, the leader had gathered around him, mostly from the Presbyterians, a number of ministers of "light and leading," who became powerful and successful evangelists of the new movement. These men went forth and boldly preached the sufficiency of the Gospel to save men, and that the testimony of God was designed and able to produce faith. "The people appeared," says Mr. Stone, "as just awakened from the sleep of ages; they seemed to see for the first time that they were responsible beings, and that the refusal to use the means appointed was a damning sin."

Many converts were made, and numerous churches established,

notably in central Kentucky and the Western Reserve of Ohio. These churches were founded on the Bible, in the plain and obvious import of its words, as the only and sufficient rule of faith and life. The designating title chosen, both for individual members and congregations, was "Christian."

Some years ago in examining the early records of the church in Cynthiana, organized by T.M. Allen in 1828, the charter written by Mr. Allen, an associate of Mr. Stone, was found in words like these, as near as they can be reproduced from memory: "We, the undersigned, wish to form ourselves into a church of our Lord and Savior Jesus Christ in the Town of Cynthiana, Ky. The name Christian is the only name by which we desire to be called, and the Bible alone is the all-sufficient rule of our faith and practice." Such were the distinguishing elements of these new Christian churches.

Union of Stone and Campbell Forces

At the time of the union of the Stone and Campbell forces in Kentucky in the year 1832, both sides were ripe and ready for the consummation. The two leaders had carried on a lengthy correspondence in their respective papers with a view of ascertaining definitely points of agreement, and differences, if any existed. There was absolute harmony in fundamentals. The aims and purposes of the two reformations were identical. Only a single minor point of variance appeared in the field of theology, and that was in regard to the effect of the atonement on God. Mr. Campbell insisted on an intellectual explanation of the atonement in its relation to the divine government, in the matter that God, as a moral governor, was enabled thereby to be just while the justifier of those who believe in Jesus. Mr. Stone declined to follow in any speculative or philosophical effort to explain the mystery of the cross in its relation to God; simply contenting himself with the everlasting yea of its acknowledged effect as the reconciler of man to God, and not God to man. This question was eliminated from the discussion as of no particular significance to either side.

The Immersion Question Settled

As most of the "New Lights," as outsiders called them, were Paedobaptists at the beginning, including the leader, the question of baptism had to be taken in hand, and threshed out to a finish. The adoption of the Bible as the only and all-sufficient rule of faith and practice, as with the two Presbyterian Campbells, at the beginning of their movement, the problem of baptism had to come up for reconsideration and final solution. It came up, and was settled in the same old way, as it always must, under similar circumstances; Mr. Stone, and an overwhelming majority of his associates, were immersed and infant baptism was relegated to the shades. Those that held out and were satisfied with affusion were so few as to constitute a negligible quantity, when the negotiations for union were finally settled, and the union consummated. This was not an instance of union by legislation of ecclesiastical authority, for neither party believed in the right of churches to legislate or command. When leading congregations of the two bodies in centers of population like Lexington, Paris, Georgetown, Richmond and Mayesville, came together, as they did, it was an easy matter for the smaller churches and individuals to fall in line.

Dr. Richardson in his **Life of Alexander Campbell** says of the Christian Connection: "They were characterized by a simplicity of belief and manners, and a liberality of spirit highly captivating, and possessed, in general, a striking and praiseworthy readiness to receive additional light from the Bible."

It is hardly worth-while to record the fact for information, that a body of "irreconcilables" refused to come into the union, and continued a separate existence under the old name. These have developed into a communion of respectable proportions, which has inherited and maintained many of the excellencies of its illustrious founder and his first associates.

Our Inheritance from Mr. Stone

In addition to the name Christian, the combined movement has inherited from Mr. Stone and his fellow-workers a larger measure of the spirit of New Testament evangelism and individual consecration of life. These reformers were mighty men of God. The intellectual and argumentative tinge of the Campbell movement needed relief by the influence of the spirit of holiness and prayer. Campbell men were didactic, exegetic, and logical; the Stone men were dynamic, explosive, and hortatory.

Campbell and Stone Compared

The combination of these qualities was needed on both sides. After the union, evangelists, as a rule, went out by twos. The Campbell man was the preacher who turned on the light, the Stone man was the exhorter who poured in the fire. A team, for instance, like Aylett Rains and John Allen Gano, what mighty engineering for the Kingdom of God! Rains, according to the colored preacher, "argufied" and Gano "brought on the arousement." An as old mountain preacher once said to the writer, "Come and go on a preaching tower (tour) with me. You'll lighten and I'll thunder, and we'll bring 'em in." The Campbell preacher lightened and the Stone evangelist thundered, and they "brought 'em in." What the intellectual and theological teaching of the "Disciples" most needed was the spiritual and hortatory element brought in by the "Christians." May this union be forever indissoluble.

WALTER SCOTT
Masterful Preacher and Teacher

THE big four of the current reformation are Thomas Campbell, Alexander Campbell, Barton W. Stone and Walter Scott. The last named is fourth in enumeration, but by no means fourth in distinctive importance. In originality of conception, vigor of presentation, enthusiasm, courage, boldness and eloquence, he comes near heading the list. He was not the initiator or representative of any organized movement within the church like his three illustrious comrades, but so far as the distinctiveness of his contributions to the new movement was concerned, he stands first in historical and theological importance.

Biographical Sketch of Scott

Mr. Scott, as his name indicates, was a Scotchman, and none the worse for that. Theology and the religious consciousness run in the blood north of the Tweed. Brains and reverence and appreciation of Biblical knowledge appear to be congenital with the typical Scotchman. Walter Scott, like the Campbells from Presbyterian north of Ireland, had inherited the best instincts and qualities of his race. Educated on his native heath, he came, in his early manhood, to the United States. An Episcopalian by affiliation and not by conviction, he came back to the traditional communion of his fathers, and took membership with a Presbyterian church soon after his arrival in this country. He had been trained for a teacher in his native land, and soon after coming to Pittsburgh, took educational work in connection with an academy in that city. He became tutor in several private families, teaching in the home of the father of Dr. Robert Richardson. Robert, the son, became his most famous pupil, studying New Testament Greek and the classics under the brilliant young Scotchman. It seems to have been his association with the Richardson's that brought him into contact with the Campbells and many other friends of the reformation in Pittsburgh. His deep religious nature, his love of truth and righteousness, his keen perception, his fine capacity for the acquisition of knowledge, and his profound reverence for the Bible and the Christian religion, made him a splendid subject for instruction and inspiration on the part of the two reformers. One of the finest passages in Dr. Richardson's **Memoirs of Alexander Campbell** is a description of the personality and powers of Walter Scott in comparison and contrast to those of Mr. Campbell, showing how one man reinforced and supplemented the other in a combination the most efficient and powerful that could be imagined in the leadership and propagation of the restoration movement.

His Sermonic Ability

Scott was a preacher of dramatic and thrilling eloquence. When one of the pioneers who had heard him has occasion to refer to great preachers or preaching, he instinctively utters the name of Walter Scott. Isaac Errett once said in referring to a great sermon preached by Dr. Armitage of New York before one of our conventions, "I have not heard such preaching since Walter Scott."

I am reminded of what a great criminal lawyer said to me of John J. Crittenden of Kentucky, and his matchless oratory. "John J.," said he, "why, at his worst he could beat 'em all, and at his best he could beat himself." Mr. Scott was not always equal in his efforts, and perhaps at his worst could not beat 'em all, but certainly at his best he could beat himself and all the rest, into the bargain. I recall some of the old fireside conversations in our country home, when my stepfather, a preacher of the first generation of Disciples, would talk of the great preachers of our movement he had heard and known. When he came to speak of Scott, he glowed with an enthusiasm and eloquence almost equal to the master he was describing. A mighty torrential sermon on the Three Divine Missions, one hour on the Mission of Christ, one hour on the Mission of the Holy Spirit, one hour on the Mission of the Church, holding his audience spellbound to the last word! A phenomenon of preaching power in an age when long sermons were expected and customary.

His Methods of Preaching

This masterful proclaimer of the Word combined the didactic, the poetic, and the evangelistic to a degree astonishingly unusual. His mind was as straight and clear in the comprehension and explanation of facts as his emotional nature was strong and moving in his appeals to men to be reconciled to God. As a teacher he possessed illuminating powers of comparison and illustration, while his spiritual mind enabled him to interpret analogies in a way at once surprising and captivating to his students and hearers. Walking in field or forest with one of his pupils he would pluck a flower from its stem, and holding it up, would say with deep and tender feeling: "Do you know, my dear, why in the scriptures Christ is called the Rose of Sharon?" If the answer was not at once ready, he would make reply: "It is because the Rose of Sharon has no thorns." And then he would go on to dilate in rapt, poetic phrase on the beautiful traits of the Savior's character.

His Pedagogic Attitude

His chief theme of comparison and illustration, next to the glory and perfection of the Redeemer, was the order and significance of the elements of the gospel. His powers of analysis and classification were phenomenal. His pedagogic attitude to the gospel never forsook him. Sometimes he would gather around him a group of boys and proceed to construct for their benefit a little primer catechism.

"Now, boys," he would say, "let us take a nice little lesson in the blessed gospel."

After a brief drill, the boys repeating after him, he would wind up the interview in a fashion like this: "Well, boys, in what does the gospel consist?"

Answer: "In facts, commands and promises."

"How many facts?"
Answer: "Three."
"What are they?"
Answer: "Death, burial and resurrection of Christ."
"How many commands?"
Answer: "Three."
"What are they?"
Answer: "Faith, repentance and baptism."
"How many promises?"
Answer: "Three."
"What are they?"
Answer: "Remission of sins, the gift of the Holy Spirit and everlasting life."

"Now, boys," the teacher would say, "what do you do with the facts?"
Answer: "Believe them."
"What do you do with commands?"
Answer: "Obey them."
"What do you do with the promises?"
Answer: "Enjoy them."

He would then express the fervent hope that the boys would accept this simple and glorious gospel and grow up good and useful men. This luminous and comprehensive classification of gospel elements, as an effective way of presenting the subject, has made a lasting impression on the Disciple consciousness. It may be doubted if there is one of our preachers in the world, or ever was in it, no matter how progressive or scientific, or up to date, or how much of the "modern spirit" he may have thought he possessed, who has not for illustrative and simplifying purposes, made use of this arrangement of the gospel of our salvation. Its exhaustiveness has been denied, it has been modified and supplemented and interpreted into a different gospel to the one Walter Scott had in mind, but it continues to be used as a helpful method of enabling the plain man to understand and follow the way of life, and perhaps it is the one thing by which its author will be best known and longest remembered in the history of our cause.

The Exclusive Basis of Christian Union

The distinctive and fundamental contribution of Mr. Scott to the theology of the reformation was not a simple and scriptural classification of the facts, commands and promises of the gospel. Not enough has been made of the fact that he was the discoverer of a new and adequate Christology based on Peter's confession in Matt. 16:16, as the means of salvation and the exclusive basis of Christian union. The honor of the discovery and formulation and first presentation of the doctrine of the immersion of a penitent believer into the name of Father, Son and Holy Spirit in order to the remission of sins, belongs to the same source. The only conception or practice in the restoration theology that could lay claim to originality or peculiarity was this idea of the immersion of a believing penitent in the name of Jesus Christ for the remission of sins and the gift of the Holy Spirit. Immersion was familiar and baptism for the remission of sins was a doctrine of all the creeds, but the two combined in relation to the penitent believer had not been taught or practiced since the days of the apostles. Dr. Richardson, in his **Life of Alexander Campbell**, brings these points into view as achievements of Walter Scott, in a single suggestive paragraph:

"His discourse was based upon Peter's Confession, Matt. 16:16, in connection with the same apostle's answer to the inquiry: 'What shall we do?' given to the penitents on the day of Pentecost, Acts 2:38. As the lordship and glory of Christ, the Son of God, was his favorite theme, and he was, on this occasion, animated with more than usual fervor, he became most eloquent, and held the audience in a state of rapt attention as he gradually developed the power of the simple but comprehensive Christian creed—the rock which Christ announced as the foundation on which he would build his church;

the grand proposition proved by the miracles of fulfilled prophecy, supernatural wisdom, divine love, healing power, and victory over the grave, detailed by the evangelists, that men might believe, and 'believing, have life through his name.' And when he went on to show his gospel was administered in the beginning and that believers were baptized into the name and into the death of Christ, and being thus buried with him and raised again to a new life, received in this symbolic act the remission of sins and the promised Holy Spirit, which was the seal of the Christian covenant and the earnest of an eternal inheritance, his hearers, while charmed with such a novel view of the simplicity and completeness of the gospel, were, as on the former occasion, filled with doubt and wonder, and were ready to ask each other, 'How can these things be ?'"

Messianic Interpretation of Peter's Confession

To take the most important consideration first: Mr. Scott's Messianic and Christological interpretation of Peter's confession, and his eloquent insistence, with both tongue and pen, upon the glorious fact that the personality of Jesus of Nazareth, the Son of God, in his threefold office of prophet, priest and king, was the creed of Christianity, the foundation of the Church, and the basis of Christian union, far exceeds in value and significance any other contribution which has been made to religious thought and life in modern times. His principal book, "The Great Demonstration," was given to the development and emphasis of this sublime and far-reaching proposition, the fact of Christ and his place in the Christian system. The other reformers were inclined to build on the Bible as the fundamental creed, thus substituting a literary for a personal foundation. They all had glimpses of the truth, but Scott discerned with greater clearness and decision the essential fact on which supreme accent must be laid. No longer were men taught to attain salvation by believing in creeds and doctrines, but by belief in and submission to a divine human person, the one who had all power to save, and all might to redeem. Christ was the object of faith, not opinions and dogmas. Men were not to trust in institutions, ordinances, or propositions for salvation, but in Christ, the Son of God and the only Savior of men. Faith was personal conviction concerning a personal Savior, the outcome of which was personal salvation and personal character. These reformers went forth as apostles and prophets had done before them, preaching Christ and practicing faith in him and obedience to his commandments as conditions of salvation and means of Christian manhood.

Its Bearing on Christian Union

The bearing of this Christological theology on Christian union, the cardinal plank in Thomas Campbell's platform, was obvious and vital. It takes us back to Paul's declaration: "Other foundation can no man lay than that which is laid, which is Jesus Christ." The rock foundation on which Christ was to build his church was not Peter's confession as an abstract truth or proposition, but Christ himself in his essential personality as the Son of God. All the possibilities of unity focalize at this point. Men may continue to arrange, formulate, and ventilate bases of unity in efforts to realize the unification of the churches, but in the future as in the past, they will have only failure for their pains. This is not the business of men, they are not competent to its adequate performance. If they were it is not needed. The foundation is already in, the basis has been divinely submitted by the Son of God in Peter's confession at Caesarea Philippi. Are not all existing evangelical churches built on Jesus Christ, on his divinity and humanity, his personality and power to save and rule? Why, then, are they divided? Their unity is fundamental, being the unity of the faith in the Son of God; their divisions are superficial, consisting of walls, like the Jews built round the law, separating each section ecclesiastically from other Christian organizations. These sectional walls are made of peculiar phrases, usages, doctrines and interpretations of certain portions of Scripture. These wall materials are sometimes foundations of the denominations, but not of the church of Jesus Christ. In order, therefore, to union as well as unity these sectional partitions must be pierced, razed to the ground, or rendered innocuous as separative institutions. All the churches need to do is to recognize and realize their unity in Christ and on Christ, and to pull down or climb over their sectarian walls, which were built to promote division and prevent the union of the people of God. The evolution and application of this confession at Caesarea to the problem of union has been the work of the Disciples for at least fifty years. There is much more to come out of it.

Baptism for Remission of Sins

The story of the introduction and proclamation and first practice, by Walter Scott, of the new doctrine of baptism for the remission of sins is too familiar to be retold at length in this connection. Adamson Bentley, in a protracted meeting held for Jacob Osborne at Braceville, preached on baptism and took the same position that Mr. Campbell had presented in his debate with McCalla, affirming that it was designed to be a pledge of remission of sins. In referring to this sermon Osborne said: "Well, Brother Bentley, you have christened baptism today." "How so?" said Mr. Bentley. "You have termed it a remitting institution." "Well," rejoined Mr. Bentley, "I do not see how this conclusion is to be avoided with the Scriptures before us." "It is the truth," said Mr. Osborne, who was a great student of the Bible. Conversation with Walter Scott, in which the matter was carefully canvassed, led him subsequently to reinvestigate the whole question in the light of his Greek New Testament. In this reconsideration of the subject, be became deeply engrossed in a study of the consecutive order appropriate to the different items of the gospel, and his great powers of analysis and arrangement came to his relief, and he placed them thus: 1. Faith. 2. Repentance. 3. Baptism. 4. Remission of sins. 5. Holy Spirit. This indisputably was the Pentecostal order, and so far as we know has not been revoked or changed. Clearing up, as it did, the obscurities and perplexities in which the gospel had long been involved, it came to the mind of Walter Scott with the compelling force of new revelation. He was not long in preaching what he discovered to be the truth of God, but the enthusiasm of the prophet was not matched by the interest of the people. His testimony, as eloquent and thrilling as it was in the manner of presentation, fell on dull minds and doubting hearts. The minds of men and women were so saturated with theories of spiritual influence and a mystical miraculous regeneration, and hereditary total depravity, that it was next to impossible for them to understand a simple, straightforward, intelligible gospel, like the one the preacher was urging upon their acceptance.

A Unique Conversion

On one occasion that turned out to be historic, near the close of a masterful exposition of the subject, a stranger came into the house and took his seat in the audience. He heard none of the sermon except a brief summary and recapitulation and a few words of invitation in which the speaker quoted Acts 2:38 and urged his hearers to come forward and be baptized for the remission of sins. The stranger, Mr. Wm. Amends by name, walked deliberately forward and asked to be baptized for remission, according to the promise of the gospel. The preacher was astounded; he did not know what to make of it; the stranger had not heard the sermon, and yet he understood the matter perfectly just as the speaker had presented it. Mr. Amends explained to Mr. Scott subsequently in a letter that has assumed a place of historic importance in Disciple literature. He had been reading the second chapter of Acts and other cases of conversion in the Acts of Apostles, and had more than once remarked to his wife that when he found a preacher who preached as Peter did on the day of Pentecost and would give the same answer to inquiring sinners as Peter did, he would be baptized and become a Christian. He was as good as his word; he embraced the first opportunity and it was as much of a surprise to him as his response was to the preacher.

The Spread and Acceptance of His Teaching

The new arrangement and interpretation of the gospel made slow progress at first, but when once the ice was fairly broken and the message understood, it went forward by leaps and bounds, especially in the Western Reserve of Ohio, where Walter Scott's first evangelistic work was done. Barton W. Stone once said to Samuel Rogers that he had preached baptism for the remission of sins at the beginning of his reformatory work, but had abandoned it because the effect was like pouring ice water down the backs of his hearers. That was because he did not preach it right, as he afterwards learned. The man who preaches immersion in its ceremonial religious aspects as a kind of juridic, legal and arbitrary external arrangement between God and the sinner, will have abundant reason to complain of a chilling effect on his audience. In the language of the old colored preacher, it will certainly have "a coolin' influence on de meetin'." But the man who puts the full, spiritual, New Testament content into the word "baptize," will not displease his most intelligent and Christian hearers. A polemic and dogmatic age gave us a lexical and controversial baptism, with about equal proportions of legalism and water mixed and generally well shaken before taken. Untold harm has been done by preaching this legalistic dogma of immersion for the remission of sins. Walter Scott and the Campbells, especially Thomas Campbell, well understood that it was not "the outward sign" and symbol that was a condition of salvation, but the "inward grace," the cleansing of the soul from sin by the power of God, compared to the action of water on a soiled garment. The symbol is put for the thing symbolized. This is the baptism that "washed away" the sins of Saul of Tarsus.

Peter explains what he meant by baptism for the remission of sins on the day of Pentecost. "The like figure whereunto baptism doth also now save us, not by the putting away of the filth of the flesh, but the answer of a good conscience toward God." It is not the physical action of immersion in water for ceremonial or bathing purposes, but the purification of the conscience from a sense of defilement and guilt by repentance and the power of God, of which the outward rite is the symbolic expression and representation. This is the historic doctrine of baptism for the remission of sins, written in all the creeds and preached by the reformers, but practiced by none of them till the time of Walter Scott and the Restoration Movement.

His Singular Unselfishness

No space remains to speak of the personal character and devotion of this great preacher of righteousness. He was a Christ-like man of singular detachment and unselfishness. A striking story of his altruism still lingers about his old haunts at Mays Lick, Ky., where he lived for a time. He had preached one of his great sermons in the presence of Alexander Campbell. At the close of the service Mr. Campbell went forward and said: "Walter, many people are complimenting you on your masterly sermon this morning. I desire to present you with a more substantial token of my appreciation," handing him a five dollar gold piece. Mr. Scott thanked him and thrust the coin into his vest pocket without looking at it. They went into the country that day to dine with one of the brethren. Riding along the road on horseback, Walter still expatiating on one of the great themes of the gospel, they encountered a beggar who made a piteous appeal for alms. The eloquent talker paused long enough to take the coin out of his pocket and give it to the tramp, again without looking at it. "Are you aware of the denomination of that piece of money you gave the beggar?" said Mr. Campbell, a few moments later, "No, no," said Walter; "was it the coin you gave me in the church?" "Yes," said Mr. Campbell, "and it was a five dollar gold piece." Here was a man who did not think of himself, only of the holy cause and of other people.

ISAAC ERRETT
Major Prophet of the Second Generation of Disciples

IN the longest personal conversation I ever had with Isaac Errett he related two circumstances of the early movement in Pittsburgh, so characteristic and typical that they may be used as illuminating side lights of his first religious environment, and the trend of the religious movement with which he had identified himself. The time was the early 30's of the last century when the "reformed church," as it was then called, began to segregate itself into a distinct religious body, separate and apart from all existing denominations of Christians. In the enthusiasm of an extreme literalism, the brethren practiced the "holy kiss" in those days.

An Incident with a Definite Result

One bright Sunday morning a big, black, burly negro man strode forward, presenting himself for membership in the church at Pittsburgh, where Brother Errett was then a member. It was the custom to march round single file, extending the right hand of congratulation and fellowship to the new convert, imprinting, at the same time, a resounding holy kiss on his glowing cheek. When the time came for the usual performance to begin on behalf of the brother in black, no one moved. Impassive, unresponsive, statuesque and cold, the people sat, reminding one of a wilderness of marble slabs in an English graveyard, until the situation became intolerably embarrassing and painful. When sensitive brethren began to feel like looking around for holes in the floor through which to escape, a maiden sister of uncertain age rushed to the front, impulsively embraced her colored brother, implanting a fervent kiss on his dusky cheek, shouting as she did so. "I will not deny my brother his privilege." "That," said Brother Errett, "put an end to the holy kiss in the Pittsburgh church."

We agreed that two obvious inferences were to be drawn from

this incident. First, that the truth of the universal brotherhood of humanity, regardless of race, color, creed, social caste, or previous condition of servitude, had not found its way into the consciousness of the brotherhood at that early stage of its history; and secondly, that extreme literalism in the interpretation of Scripture that makes a social custom of the ancient East as binding as a vital truth of the gospel, is decidedly superficial. It passes into "innocuous desuetude" at the first touch of the stress and strain of life.

The second story referred to an election of elders that had taken place in the same church. The qualifications of church officers was a burning question in those days. So rigid and literal was the construction put upon the qualifications of elders in Timothy that it was always difficult and sometimes impossible to find men to fill the office. On this particular occasion, the church had put in some of its best men to serve it in the capacity of bishops. Satisfaction with the results of the election was general but not universal. An old Scotchman in the congregation complained that the Scriptures had not been carried out. The men put in were not qualified to do the work of the eldership. Walking home with his family that day, he growled his criticisms all the way. He was not "satisfied" with what had been done. "Brother A. was all but unanimously elected," said his wife: "what's the matter with him?" "He's not qualifeed," said the old Scot. "Brother B. is a most excellent and capable man; what's the trouble with him?" "He's na qualifeed." She named another and another, and the same old answer came back, "He's na qualifeed." Piqued somewhat at the carping attitude of the tough old Scot, the good wife indignantly asked, "Who, then, is qualifeed?" "I am," he replied, with a crashing guttural accent on the broad a of the word "am."

The new democracy always takes care of the individuality of its citizens. Where the way is made for liberty, the self-conscious ego runs and is glorified. It is the way of new movements to attract egoistic cranks and hoary-headed malcontents, men born in the objective case and active voice, the kind that foregathered with David in the cave of Adullam. Our early history had its share of this species of the genus homo, who are always at home on questions of church organization and government.

The Founding of The Christian Standard

Isaac Errett's leadership of our reformatory' movement began with the first issue of the *Christian Standard* in March, 1866. Previous to the time of this publication he had won distinction as a man of commanding power with both tongue and pen. "The Living Pulpit of the Christian Church," edited by W.T. Moore and published in 1868, begins a brief biographical sketch of Isaac Errett with these two sentences:—"Among the preachers and writers of the nineteenth century who have plead for a return to primitive Christianity, the subject of this notice stands pre-eminently among the most distinguished. For more than thirty-five years he has been connected with the Disciples, and, during the greater portion of that time, has been an earnest, able and successful advocate of their plea for reformation."

He Proves His Breadth and Power

The ancient and potent laws of heredity, environment and training, that made Saul of Tarsus the great interpreter and expounder of Jesus in the first generation of Christianity, made Isaac Errett the most luminous exponent in the interpretation and defense of the Campbell movement, for the time in which he lived. His aptitude as a scholar and his early and intimate association with the Campbells and Walter Scott, gave him exceptional opportunities to understand and appreciate the aims and ideals of the "current reformation." His great sermon in the "Living Pulpit" on "The Law of Progressive Development," placed him in the front rank of progressive and liberal interpreters of the restoration plea. It soon became evident in the conduct of the Standard that its editor was too large to be small, too broad to be narrow, too deep to be shallow, too clear and keen and penetrating of vision to be satisfied with a sectarian conception of Christianity while pleading for its opposite. People who fight sectarianism acquire, as a rule, the spirit of a sectarian, and those who would overthrow denominationalism find themselves obsessed by a first-class instance of denominational consciousness. When the limitations of human nature bump against the problems of theology, there is apt to be a potent illustration of the saying of Douglas Jerrold, that dogmatism is puppyism come to maturity. Lutherans of the second generation were as intolerant and persecuting as the Catholics who tried to stamp them out in the first. A dogmatic age begets dogmatism in those who set themselves to oppose dogma, and the spirit of controversy is sure to aggravate extreme tendencies.

It was hardly to be expected that Disciple human nature should differ from the human nature of other people, or that they should be less influenced by environment and the temper of the age than their contemporaries.

Alexander Campbell, Number One, of the covenant theology, the Lochian philosophy, and the third epistle of Peter, who stressed the objective in revelation, the external and hence the institutional in religion, begat a spiritual progeny in his own image and after his own likeness, who ran ahead of their maker in a hard, mechanical and quarrelsome legalism, which they sought to fasten as a yoke upon the necks of their brethren. The most popular and authoritative and serviceable passage of Scripture used by these men who esteemed themselves "infallibly right" was the familiar declaration: "Where the Scriptures speak we speak, and where the Scriptures are silent we are silent," and this was the result of a strict constructionism, the principle of which they applied in the interpretation of other Scriptures.

The Organ Controversy

About the time of the beginning of the *Christian Standard*, a fierce and internecine war broke out on the subject of instrumental music in the services of the church; another product of negative literalism. When the proposal was made to put the organ in as an aid to the service of song, it was met by the objection that the introduction of musical instruments into the house of God was a sin comparable to the golden calf in the camp of Israel or infant sprinkling in the modern church. It was idolatry and will worship because the New Testament is silent concerning it, and there is no "thus saith the Lord" authorizing its use in the house of God. Isaac Errett through his paper did yeoman service in educating our people up to the point of realizing that this kind of reasoning was a serious abuse of the whole question of divine authority in the Holy Scriptures. A purblind legalism and a cocksure dogmatism were making a desperate struggle to head the movement in the wrong direction. "The old reliable," the pet name of the American Christian Review, had gone over to the firing line of anti-ism, and opened its batteries on missionary societies, the organ, the one-man pastor, all progressive tendencies, and everybody's sectarianism but its own. It is impossible for men and women of our day who are clambering into the band-wagon of progress, both in politics and religion, to comprehend the fact that a little more than a generation back the word "progress" and all its derivatives were under ban, among religious reformers too, and the most damning thing that could be said of a man was that he was a "progressive."

The Parting of the Ways

Times change, and so do men when they can be persuaded to think. There was a prophetic and providential line of lineal descendants from Alexander Campbell, Number Two, of the *Millennial Harbinger*, Lunenburgh letter, and the presidential chair of the American Christian Missionary Society. Men of the type of Isaac Errett, Robert Richardson, W.K. Pendleton, W.T. Moore, J.S. Lamar, Alexander Procter, Geo. W. Longan, and others of similar caliber, broadly intellectual as they were broadly spiritual, were in the true prophetic succession from Thomas Campbell and the matured and fully developed Alexander Campbell. At the time of the death of the Sage of Bethany and the birth of the *Christian Standard*, these events occurred the same month, March, 1866, it was a serious question as to which way the cat was going to jump. The two tendencies had reached the parting of the ways, and the choice lay between hardening into a legalistic and belligerent sect, or marching into the upward and onward way of a catholic and spiritual interpretation of New Testament religion.

Isaac Errett was called to the kingdom for such a time as this. His relation to the Campbell movement was similar to Paul's relation to the Christianity of Jesus and the Holy Spirit, when he saved it from being strangled in its cradle by Jewish legalists, and buried in the tomb of a decadent Leviticism, and set it in the highway of holiness as the faith of mankind. If the religion of Jesus needed interpretation and re-adaptation to changing conditions in the first generation of its existence, it is not strange that reform wrought by human hands should need the touch of reconstruction and fresh leadership in its second generation. When a forward step is taken, or changing readjustments occur, the old battle for freedom of thought and action has to be fought over again. New religious movements reach finality and crystallize in less than a generation. They fought for liberty to overthrow the old order and gained it, but they will not grant a similar privilege to their contemporaries and those who come after them. The last word has been spoken and woe be to the man who dares to speak another—he must be prepared to take the consequences.

One of his first efforts was to break up the crystallization into which the cause was rapidly drifting. The tendency to externalize Christianity by spelling it out in institutions and writing it into abstract propositions, supported by texts of Scripture, superficially interpreted, was deplored. We were inclined to forget the important distinction so carefully drawn by the Campbells between faith and opinion, fact and speculation, experience and dogma. The disposition to lead people out of the synagogue, not for lack of faith, or any deficiency in their experience of the grace of God, but for paltry differences of opinion, of little importance in themselves, was not esteemed a part of the primitive Christianity for whose restoration we were proudly contending. The age of polemics and dogmatic literalism did not end with Isaac Errett and the day of his editorship of the *Christian Standard*, but a better and broader spirit began to characterize our literature and the attitude of our people towards other religious bodies.

"What Is Sectarianism?"

Perhaps the most illuminating contribution ever made to a Disciple periodical was the article written by the editor of the Standard to Moore's *Christian Quarterly* entitled, "What is Sectarianism?" This essay was a masterpiece of exposition, throwing as it did a flood of light on the fundamental principles of the restoration cause. It was the Declaration and Address revised and brought up to date, another stage of evolution brought in, by the operation of the law of progressive development. It had been the custom to invite men and women to unite with us on the Bible and the Bible alone as the religion of Protestants. This, of course, was an invitation to union on the basis of our interpretation of certain portions of the Bible, a foundation no more adequate or satisfactory than the creeds proposed by the founders of other religious bodies. No human interpretation of literary documents, inspired or uninspired, could be made the foundation of the church or a basis of the reunion of the churches. Walter Scott's Christology, based on the inspired confession at Caesarea Philippi, was farther expounded and applied in some of its most important implications. The "rock" on which the church was to be erected was not a proposition or an institution, but a person, and that person was Christ himself. The divinity and personality of Jesus of Nazareth, the object of faith, the power of salvation, the foundation of the church, the basis of Christian union, the inspiration of the Christian life, the essence of the Christian religion, constitutes the rallying center of all those in every place who call upon His name. Other things, if in any way vital, may go into the structure, but not into the foundation. The Disciples have often been spoken of as creedless, but this is a serious misapprehension of our position. Creedlessness is not one of our limitations. The Bible is a source of spiritual knowledge, a practical rule in the guidance of our lives, but Christ is the creed of Christianity, the creed that needs no revision, and no apology. If the Disciples, at any time, have proposed a theory of primitive Christianity and the ancient order of things as the basis of unity, they have been as much mistaken as others who have offered human theories for the fact of Christ. Having no claim to inerrancy, above other people, it is probable that some things have gone into the foundation that belonged elsewhere, but at the same time steady progress is being made towards the realization of the ideal of unity in and on the Son of God and Son of man, alone.

Approved by Present Day Leaders of Thought

To those of us who sat at the feet of Isaac Errett and other great teachers of the time, it is a matter of intense gratification that the profoundest and most up-to-date thinking of these modern days is falling into line with the Christological position of our restoration cause. A notable book has just appeared in Germany, from the pen of Dr. Sapper, one of the great thinkers and scholars of the Fatherland, entitled, "The New Protestantism," in which he repeats and amplifies with signal ability and force, the thesis of the great *Quarterly* article to which I am referring in this paper. He declares in refreshing Disciple style that theological questions are being pushed into a secondary place, and it is the work of the leaders of the New Protestantism to define and lay down those principles of evangelical religion which unite rather than divide Christians. He then reaches for the milk of the cocoanut in this declaration: "All that is necessary is contained in the formulary belief in Jesus Christ as our Redeemer. This is the essence of the Christian religion, and there is no other essence."

Arthur Bransewetter, a careful and temperate writer and able reviewer, recognizes this and admits that Sapper's book is directed to unite Christians in all that is great and essential in their religion. "We must," says Bransewetter, "under all circumstances and at any price find a central point around which we can congregate," and that point is the personality of Jesus Christ, our Brother and our Redeemer.

Dr. Newton Marshall, one of the most brilliant and scholarly preachers in England, who died recently at the early age of forty, insisted in some of his last utterances "that Christianity was central to all religions, and a personal Christ was the central fact of Christianity."

The people who have been contending for a return to Christ will have to hurry up or some of these outside men will beat them to a full and practical application of our divine creed to the solution of the problems of unity and the world's redemption. . One of the most vital questions growing out of the contention for the centrality and fundamentality of Jesus as prophet, priest, and king, was the exclusion of things that did not belong to the "essence" and the inclusion of things that did. That, indeed, is the problem of the New Protestantism of which Sapper speaks. One of the first things to be considered is the terms of Christian fellowship and brotherhood, things that must be believed and done in this new reign of God over the lives of men. We must penetrate to the essence of what the personality of Jesus incarnates, "the life of God in the soul of man." According to the testimony of Christ himself and that of his inspired apostles, two things only are indispensable, faith in Christ as Savior, and obedience to Him as Lord. In the nature of things the forms of religion do not and can not belong to its essence. Institutional and sacramental religion belongs at best to the category of expression, not to that of substance or the things expressed. On the preaching of the apostles they required nothing of men but belief in Christ, the human life of God, and submission to the eternal law of righteousness, of which he was the manifestation. As long as men maintained the integrity of their faith in Jesus and their loyalty to him as the Son of God, they were sound in the faith and members of his body, the church. On these simple conditions men came in and stayed in regardless of their opinions and speculations on a thousand questions, not affecting attachment and devotion to Jesus the Christ of God.

Mr. Errett's Statement of the Restoration Plea

Mr. Errett thus sums up the restoration plea:

1. "It insists on faith in Jesus as the Messiah, the Son of God, as the only condition of admission to baptism and membership in the church."
2. "It enjoins obedience to Jesus, the Head of the Church, as the only condition of fellowship in the church."
3. "It advocates the union of all believers on these two considerations: Faith in Jesus; obedience to Jesus—thus letting party names and organizations and creeds give place to a spiritual brotherhood which, possessed of whatever diversity of opinion or of practice outside the simple teachings of the New Testament, shall be one in faith and in character as the followers of the Lord Jesus Christ."

In no sphere of influence did Isaac Errett exhibit more wisdom and usefulness than in the realm of liberty, tolerance, and expediency. "In all matters," said he, "outside of faith in Christ and obedience to him, there were two regulations. First, no one was allowed to judge his brother. Every one was at liberty to follow his own best judgment, responsible only to God. Second, if this liberty was found, in the exercise, to work to the injury of any brother, however weak, or to disturb the peace and harmony of the church, they were taught to waive their rights and restrain their liberties, in loving deference to the prejudices or weaknesses of their brethren. The reader is referred to Romans XIV for a luminous exposition of the Christian law of love in its application to all such cases."

Features of the New Testament Church

The features of the New Testament Church to be restored, or reproduced in our time, are first, its ecumenical character. It was the holy catholic church, exhausted by no sect or denomination, belonging to no country, nation, or class. Second, its universal equality. It has no hierarchy, or priestly order. It is a great spiritual brotherhood bound by spiritual ties of faith, hope and love, and depends not on organization for its unity; its unity is from within, and not without— unity of spirit, and not a mere external unity of organization. Third, the simplicity and brevity of its creed. It contained but one article of faith. It came from heaven. "Thou art the Christ, the Son of the living God." Fourth, the simple bond of fellowship that held its members together. Devotion to Jesus and consecration to the spirit of love and obedience. For two reasons only could men and women be rightfully cut off from the fellowship of the saints; first, for denying the Lord that bought them, thereby renouncing the divine creed; second, for persistent disobedience to the authority of the head of the church. If they were right here, no matter how far wrong they might be in anything else, their fellowship could not be disturbed; if they were wrong here, no matter if right about everything else, they forfeited their right to Christian brotherhood and were delivered over to the world.

The Ideal New Testament Church

In the two following items he summed up his conception and interpretation of the effort to realize the ideal Christianity and the ideal church of the New Testament.

1. "We must guard, with uncompromising integrity, the es-

sentials of this plea, namely, faith in the Lord Jesus, and obedience to him in all things clearly taught in his word.

2. "We must carefully guard, and with an equally uncompromising faithfulness to principle, against all attempts to coerce unity, either in regard to inferential truths or matters of expediency. That is to say, while insisting on loyalty to Jesus, we must allow every man to be loyal to himself in all things not expressly commanded or taught, and regard this liberty as his right and not as our gift."

MOSES E. LARD

Prophet of Radicalism, Literalism, and Conservatism in the Second Generation of the Restoration Movement

As a thinker, writer, preacher, defender of the faith, mighty advocate and propagandist of the new cause of Christian union, few men of the middle period equaled, and none surpassed, the man whose name stands at the head of this article. The genius of Alexander Campbell and the impelling force of the principles he had sent out, as a bugle call to the churches, drew around him in Bethany College a group of young men of superior talents and consuming zeal, the very best of raw material for the making of able and successful ministers of the word. Like our Lord's "Winnowing Sieve," spoken of by Prof. Seely in his brilliant "Ecce Homo," the sieving and winnowing process sifts out the light material and retains the best of the wheat in the first and second generations of a new cause. The men who were trained by Alexander Campbell, like the old students of the great Agassiz, always speak of him in the glow of a passionate enthusiasm, indicating a capacity for the understanding and appreciation of genius not always to be distinguished from genius itself.

Great Men of Our Second Period

Great men multiply themselves in other men, a kind of self-multiplication by inspiration. For a whole generation and more a strong force of men of capacity and personality went out from Bethany, who give to the Christian Union Reformation a permanent place among the religious forces of the world. Of these captains of a new spiritual industry, with no less an ambition than the reunion of Christendom on a divine basis, were such men as Dr. Robert Richardson, W.K. Pendleton, C.L. Loos, Robert Graham, Moses E. Lard, John W. McGarvey, J.S. Lamar, W.T. Moore, L.B. Wilkes, William Baxter, John Shackelford, Henry Haley, Joseph King; and besides these other men of light and leading, who came under the influence and teaching of the illustrious head of Bethany College, Isaac Errett, L.L. Pinkerton, Robert Milligan, Dr. W.H. Hopson, and others of both classes, too numerous to mention here.

Moses Lard, Preacher

A book of surpassing interest and importance to the Disciples might be written on these representative men of the second stage in the evolution of our religious movement. For our present purpose, only three or four of these leaders can be considered, and they as types of personality and teaching ability characteristic of the period. Moses E. Lard represented a phase of the Disciple reformation, which has changed since his day, and we need to know something of the background out of which these changes have been proceeding. As these articles are not primarily biographical, we cannot linger over the details of his personal life in the development of his character, as interesting and valuable as these would be. We must begin with him in the maturity of his powers, in the midst of his career, as a great advocate of our reformatory principles.

As a preacher he had few equals, and no superiors, among his contemporaries. I have heard nearly all of the supreme masters of the pulpit in the English speaking world, in the last generation and a half, and I have never heard a better preacher than Moses E. Lard.

Dr. Winthrop H. Hopson, Lard's greatest rival for pulpit supremacy among the Disciples at the time, was once asked, which was the better preacher, himself or Moses Lard. The answer was, "Up to thirty sermons Lard can beat anybody, after that, up to two hundred and fifty, I can beat him." This question had brass enough in it on the part of the questioner, but the answer was characteristic of Dr. Hopson, and a pretty accurate judgment of the relative merits of the two preachers. Like Walter Scott, Lard was not always at his best, and his efforts therefore were not always equal. His average sermons as a pastor did not measure up to the special efforts on which he had spent his life. The major part of his ministry was spent in the evangelistic field, where thirty or forty great sermons were enough to give his work the highest efficiency, in a day when great preaching was expected and appreciated. The labor bestowed upon these "big sermons" was colossal. Such thoroughness of preparation, such mastery of material, I have never known in any preacher. Every phrase and sentence was fixed and set in order, and so familiar that his mind gamboled and bounded over the matter of his discourse with a freedom that gave unusual vitality and power to his utterances. The effects were sometimes electrical.

His Oratorical Power

He himself gave a specific instance of the overwhelming power of these tidal waves of eloquence. He does not refer to himself as the speaker, but he was, all the same:

"The breathless stillness of the great crowd was at times oppressive and painful. You felt as if you wanted to see the crowd move, wanted some sign of life—anything, in a word, to relieve the petrified scene before you. Had you entered a room in some buried city where a whole audience had perished in an instant, where the spirits had left the bodies fresh as in life, with the hue on the cheek, the sparkle in the eye, and the thought on the brow, little more could you have felt the awe-inspiring stillness than in the silent audience before you. Only on one occasion did the emotion rise so high as to be overpowering. At the close of one of the exhortations, even Mason Summers was mute. He could not sing a word. Several tried, but all failed. So overwhelming was the feeling that every tongue and note was hushed. Here and there a deep drawn breath or bursting sigh was all that could be heard. Men stood and looked like statues weeping. First one and then another would rise and come forward to confess his faith in Christ, until twelve strong men sat on the front seat. Such a sight I have never seen before; I have not seen it since. Glad hearts were in that audience that night, but far too full to talk. Men thought but thought in silence; felt, but never spoke. Even after the crowd adjourned, they glided over the roads homeward through the deep shadows of primitive woods noiselessly, as if they had been troops of spectres marching to their last doom. Even Gill for the time ceased to bray, while Huffaker was mute and walked clerically. The sects grew sullen, bigots gnashed, even the wizard spirit of Collet Haynes was dumb, and it is believed that any rake in the neighborhood might, for the time, have climbed one of Andy Fuller's saplings without the fear of presentment to the grand jury."

For appreciation of local references to characters like Gill, Huffaker and Collet Haynes, the reader is referred to "'Solomon's Confession," in *"Lard's Quarterly"* for October, 1864. It is worth looking up if one has access to it.

The Story of the Pioneer

I have, myself, witnessed scenes in the preaching of this great pulpiteer similar to the one described, as occurring at Haynesville, Mo. I have seen great audiences, when the invitation was given, sit paralyzed, apparently unable to move hand or foot or faculty of the mind. Not infrequently an exhortation had to be delivered by some one else, to liberate the forces of reaction and bring the people back to consciousness of their power to sing or walk forward to make the good confession. No speaker of my knowledge could bring as many handkerchiefs into requisition, or make people sob aloud as if their hearts would break. I witnessed, as many others did, an unforgettable incident, in connection with the delivery of his graphic and thrilling sermon on the Wilderness Temptation of our Lord. Speaking of the suffering of the hunger-lust of a forty days' fast and the human impossibility of it beyond fourteen days, without miraculous interposition, he drew an illustration from the experience of a Missouri hunter, from whose lips he had heard the story.

This pioneer tiller of the soil was in the habit of traveling a distance from home, at least once a year, on a hunting expedition. On this particular forage after wild game he had taken with him, his horse, his little son, his faithful dog, and a partial supply of food. After a camping place had been selected, the tent put up, and other preparations made, the hunter was priming his gun, when it accidentally went off, the bullet tearing into his body a serious if not fatal wound. Far from help and home the situation was desperate if not irremediable. There was nothing left but for the boy to take the horse and try to find his way back home to tell what had happened, and if possible to bring or send relief. The little fellow was solemnly charged not to try to guide the horse, but to drop the reins on the animal's neck and trust to his instincts of direction to find the way. He had not traveled very far when he began to feel that the horse had made a mistake. He seized the reins and turned him in the opposite direction and—was lost. If I remember correctly it was more than a week before he reached his home.

In the meantime the wound was little better and the suffering man could not supply himself with food. Morning and evening the faithful dog went out on the surrounding hills and howled by the hour that relief might come to his dying master. No relief came. On the morning of the fourteenth day the dog came in for the last time and, lying down by his human friend, he seemed to say, Well, master, I have done my best, I hope relief will yet come. If it does not we will starve and die together. The wounded man, in a fit of hunger and desperation, seized his knife and struck his heroic and devoted companion dead at his feet. As he lay there weltering in the blood of a tragic sacrifice, specks appeared on the horizon like birds, which turned out on nearer approach to be men on horses; a search-party had been organized to bring relief to their unfortunate neighbor. The hunter was rescued and recovered, but he never forgave himself the tragic end of the more than human friend, the faithful dog.

I have not told this story half as well as Lard told it, and perhaps some of the details are not correctly stated, but this is the tale substantially as he related it, and the effect was magical and unforgettable. Tears literally rained down the faces of the people, and they wept aloud all over the house. The speaker paused thirty seconds or more and then said, in substance, as far as I can recall it from memory: Yes, when I tell you of the accidental wounding of a hunter and the death of his dog, you shed copious tears, and weep like your last friend had been taken from you, but when I speak of the broken heart of my Lord, who was wounded for our transgressions and bruised for our iniquities, who was torn and tortured upon the accursed tree, without a remedy to deaden his pains, or a friendly hand to give him a drink of water, you sit unmoved by the world tragedy of God's dying Son on the cross, not a tear falls, not a sigh or sob is heard, not one heart is broken—brethren, what do you think of yourselves?

At the moment of the falling of this thunderbolt the brethren were not thinking much of themselves. Other tears were shed, but they were tears of humiliation when the fact was thrust into their consciousness that they had allowed familiarity with the most moving story ever told to rob it of its power to touch the heart and move the soul.

Spontaneous Appreciation

Old "Uncle Si Collins," as he was called, an eccentric but godly and consecrated pioneer preacher, of Richmond, Ky., who was in the habit of standing on the margin of a stream or pool when the holy ordinance of baptism was being administered, as the candidate was being lowered beneath the yielding wave, would shout, "Farewell, vain world, I'm going home"—this grand old man was a great admirer of Moses E. Lard. He would ride many miles on horseback, over dirt roads, in all kinds of weather to hear his favorite preacher. Once when Lard was holding a protracted meeting in Winchester, old Uncle Si sat by the side of his friend William

Azbill, listening to one of the speaker's greatest efforts. The orator was in one of his happiest moods. As he reached for one of his most telling climaxes, it was evident that Uncle Si was rapidly filling up. He leaned forward smiling and nodding his approval, he slapped his knees, he clapped his hands, and when, like Job's friend, he had reached the bursting point and could contain himself no longer, he turned half way round in his seat, brought down his open hand on the shoulder of his companion, and shouted out loud in meetin', "Brother Bill, isn't he a sugar stick!" So he was in these great sunbursts of sacred eloquence, in which, like John J. Crittenden, in a different field, "he could beat himself."

Lard's Fame as a Writer

His fame as a writer was scarcely second to his reputation as a preacher. He leaped suddenly into literary and polemical renown one morning, when his book entitled "A Review of Campbellism Examined" came out. Dr. Jeremiah B. Jeter, a knight of the quill in Baptist Israel, indicted a somewhat pretentious volume, under the offensive name of "Campbellism Examined." This book was able and scholarly, but marred by serious misapprehension, if not misrepresentation, of the reunion plea. Mr. Campbell began a review of it in the *Millennial Harbinger*, but being unable to finish the job through press of other duties, handed the Baptist editor and his beloved bantling over to the tender mercies of young Lard, then a recent graduate of Bethany College. The "Review" had its limitations in the temper and spirit of the reviewer, and in historical knowledge and exegesis of Scripture on a few points, but for the chief end and purpose of the book, nothing more was left to be said. The opposition suffered overthrow and rout, almost equal to annihilation, calling to mind the more recent parallel of Lambert's Notes on Ingersoll, in which the priest so completely annihilates the infidel as not to leave two tips of tails tied together and a little fur, reminders of the historic battle of the Kilkenny cats. The remorseless logic and brilliant rhetoric brought to bear by the reviewer in the defeat of his opponent, was freely admitted by many Baptists, who deplored the censorious and uncharitable spirit in which the work had been done. Years later Bro. Lard said to a friend of mine. "If I had left out the caustic and bitter things said in that book it would have been much stronger and certainly more Christian." While nothing can be said in justification of biting sarcasm, which Thomas Carlyle declared was the language of the devil, something can be said in palliation of the offense under the circumstances in which the Review of "Campbellism Examined" was written. At that time, not so long ago, the furnace of theological strife was heated seven times, like the one through which the Hebrew children passed, with this difference: four men who essayed to pass through the former came out without the smell of fire upon their garments; whereas, when one man attempted to pass through the latter when Moses E. Lard was fireman, he barely managed to get out with the smell of cooked meat and burning grease upon his skin; his garments had gone up in smoke and flame. The time had not then come for the elimination of personalities, ridicule and caustic observations from religious discussion. It has now.

Lard's Quarterly

Mr. Lard's literary career is seen to best advantage in his Quarterly, published during the Civil War. It ran through three and a half volumes, if my memory avouches correctly. Its peculiarity was, that in the neighborhood of three-fourths of its contributions were written by the editor. A noteworthy and pleasing feature of this characteristic publication was the interspersing of many theological essays and closely reasoned sermons with racy narratives, vital stories, epigrammatic delineations of character, lit up here and there with touches of the creative imagination that Charles Dickens and William Makepeace Thackeray would have found it hard to excel. The editor of the Quarterly was a matchless story-teller. He possessed the rare gifts of narration and delineation combined. Long ago such stories and histories as "My First Meeting," "Dick and South Point," "Solomon's Confession," "My Church," and a ghost story, the title of which I have forgotten, and a few other choice selections from his writings, should have been gathered into a volume as a memorial to the genius of its author. The New York Ledger, while it was publishing the star papers of Henry Ward Beecher, offered the editor of the Quarterly five thousand dollars a year to contribute similar stories to its pages. Mr. Lard wisely declined, for these productions were occasional inspirations. They could not have been made to order with the printer's devil standing at his elbow.

His Bald Literalism

Many of his great sermons were written out in the form of theological essays and published in the Quarterly. These editorial contributions to the periodical had the same verve and flash, concentrated power, note of dogmatic certainty, and bald literalism of interpretation that characterized the spoken sermons. Rarely, indeed, if ever, has any man been able to literalize the glowing symbolism of Jewish apocalypses, and dramatize them with such lurid vividness as prophetic descriptions of historic events soon to materialize in the affairs of men. Everything was literal, everything that John said in an apocalyptic drama was going to happen just as John said it. While this method yielded realistic and dramatic sermon material, as an effort to interpret spiritual prophecy it was distinctly bad. In his sermon on the New Birth in *the Living Pulpit*, Bro. Lard occupies several pages in arguing that water in John 3:5 means water. Of course it does, but does a liquid used to describe the spiritual change of repentance, mean nothing but a liquid? It must be said, however, in justice to this good man, that the spiritual and ethical elements were not lacking in either his preaching or his life. It is one of the most precious of God's providences that a man's mental concepts may be mistaken in many things, his theology all askew, when his heart is right in the sight of God, his essential message is not stripped of its saving power.

His Stand for Closed Communion

It was during the middle period or second generation of our Disciple history that many of the important problems of the new movement had to be threshed out, and, if possible, solved. The only method of threshing out things which can find acceptance among a free people is the method of public discussion. It was said of a polemic preacher of that era that he always preached from one text, a text found in one of the minor prophets: "Arise and thresh." In this particular instance the preacher, who was always ready for "'spute," threshed "the sects," but we found it necessary at times to thresh one another, that we might all find our bearing together. The most memorable internal controversy of the period was on the communion question in the pages of the *Millennial Harbinger*, *Lard's Quarterly*, and the American Christian Review. Mr. Lard stated the issue interrogatively: "Do the Unimmersed Commune?"

In an elaborate and closely reasoned article he answered this question in the negative. In this attitude of a mechanical and ceremonial interpretation of the terms of fellowship at the Lord's table, he was joined by a number of our strongest men: Geo. W. Elley, L.B. Wilkes, Dr. J.W. Cox, and Benj. Franklin, of the American Christian Review. The other side was represented by such scholarly and spiritual men as W.K. Pendleton, Isaac Errett, and Dr. Richardson in the Harbinger, and Thomas Munnell in the Quarterly. Mr. Elley thus sententiously and catechetically puts the argument for the support of the doctrine that the unimmersed do not commune:

1. Can any person be a Christian, who is not in Christ, or who has not put him on?
2. If not, can any put him on who have not been baptized "into him?"

3. Can any one be free from sin who has not, from his heart, "obeyed the form of doctrine" delivered to him by the Holy Spirit? If not, can he rightfully be allowed to break the loaf by the action of God's church?
4. Can an unsaved or unpardoned person be allowed to sit and drink the Lord's body and blood by church consent?
5. Is baptism demanded of penitents in order to pardon or Sonship?

All of these questions were answered in the negative except the last.

If Mr. Elley's restricted communion premises are admitted, the restriction of communion privileges to immersed believers necessarily follows. The trouble was his literal and legalistic process misinterpreted some of his premises.

Isaac Errett's Stand

Isaac Errett, who contributed a brilliant series of articles to this controversy in the pages of the *Millennial Harbinger*, expressed, in a letter to Richard Hawley, the conclusion which has prevailed among the Disciples. He said:

"We are compelled, therefore, to recognize as Christians many who have been in error on baptism, but who in the spirit of obedience are Christians indeed. (See Rom. 2:28, 29.) I confess, for my own part, did I understand the position of the brethren to deny this, I would recoil from my position among them with utter disgust. It will never do to unchristianize those on whose shoulders we are standing, and because of whose previous labors we are enabled to see some truths more clearly than they. Yet while fully according to them the piety and Christian standing which they deserve, it is clear that they are in great error on the question of baptism—and we must be careful not to compromise the truth. Our practice, therefore, is neither to invite nor reject particular classes of persons, but to spread the table in the name of the Lord, for the Lord's people, and allow all to come who will, each on his own responsibility."

It remains only to be added that this discussion was conducted on both sides with great ability and admirable courtesy, and was, once for all, determinative of our relations to the Christian people of the churches around us.

Lard's Opposition to Creeds

Bro. Lard's opposition to human creeds was so straight as to lean considerably beyond the perpendicular. His fierce assault on the harmless "Synopsis," a statement of principles written by Isaac Errett, for public information, is a case in point. As a matter of course the distinguished editor of the Quarterly was sublimely unconscious of the fact that in every issue of his paper he was perpetrating a creed, and many creeds, quite as human as the one he so bitterly assailed. The first sentence of his criticism has acquired a kind of historic notoriety on account of the grimness of the unconscious humor that lurks in it: "There is not a sound man in our ranks who has seen the preceding 'Synopsis' that has not felt scandalized by it." As the writer went on, the humor increased. A little farther down on the same page he declared: "When Aaron's calf came out, had he called it a bird, still all Israel seeing it stand on four legs, with horns and parted hoofs, would have shouted, a calf, a calf, a calf."

The American Christian Review joined the Quarterly in the racket against Isaac Errett, as arch-heretic and creed-maker, which caused W.T. Moore in his "History of the Disciples of Christ," to remark, "Both Mr. Lard and Benj. Franklin continued to emphasize these infinitesimal matters until it looked at one time as if the whole movement might be wrecked by an undermining of microbes." While this microbic activity did not seriously affect the main lines of the movement, it did eat the bottom out of the organ controversy. I have just laid down a volume of *Lard's Quarterly* after reading his article on "Instrumental Music in Churches, and Dancing." Notwithstanding my familiarity with the fierce intolerance of that controversial age, the consuming heat, and domineering dogmatism, implacable intolerance and bitterness of that philippic over a matter so incidental and small, I am almost surprised. We can hardly help wondering that a great man under any conditions or combination of circumstances, should fail to see the difference between secondary and insignificant matters and the loftiest fundamentals in the religion of Christ. That is one of the mysteries of sin that still gives us more or less trouble. At the same time, when we take into account the temperament and environment of the man there is not much to wonder at. He was a person of marked individuality, great intensity of conviction, and feelings so strong as to be easily fanned into a flame. As to the settlement of the organ strife, the microbes kept on eating till both gable ends and the puncheon floor of the question fell out of their own weight. In the face of preachers, editors, and ancient elders in Israel, the people quietly put the instrument in, as they had done long before in their homes. There are other things troubling our scribes the rank and file are destined to settle in the same way.

Old Age Sweetens

But the distinguished editor of the Quarterly was right on most things, and concerning the few on which he was wrong he got right before he died. As the shadows lengthened, and his western sun neared the horizon, he added sweetness to the light he had long possessed. In the last few years of his life his mind broadened in its outlook, his soul deepened in its consciousness of the love of God, and he became more tolerant, charitable and sympathetic than he had been in the heat of the strife through which he had passed. A year or two before his death he said to his old friend, J.S. Withers, of Cynthiana, Ky.: "If I had my life to live over, I would not preach another gospel, but I would preach the same gospel in a different spirit. I would not allow myself to be stranded on the desert of dogmatism and a narrow construction of the love of God, but I would preach with a new vision of its meaning, that 'God so loved the world that he gave his only begotten Son, that whosoever believeth in him should not perish, but have everlasting life.' "

WINTHROP H. HOPSON AND GEORGE W. LONGAN

Two Representative Types of Leadership in the Middle Period of Our History

In every movement of thought and life two distinct and variant types of leadership inevitably figure. It is customary to speak of these, for the want of better terms, as conservative and progressive; sometimes varied by the terms reactionary for the first and liberal or radical for the second. These words will do well enough in a loose, general way, but they are not the best of descriptive terms that could be chosen with the English language at our disposal. A more specific and discriminating classification, in my judgment, from a psychological point of view, would be the plain, familiar terms, mechanical and vital. A mechanical intellect, like any other machine, is an organization; a vital mind is an organism. They both have energy and motion, only one has life and growth.

The Mechanistic Brain

A mechanistic brain takes in ideas as a distended bladder takes in beans, or a vise grips a piece of wood. Those beans roll and rattle, becoming harder and drier in the process, till they rot, and the bladder falls to pieces from decay. Those grains of wheat found in the skull of an Egyptian mummy had been there over three thousand years, and when they rained down and rattled over the floor of the British Museum they were the same old grains of wheat, unchanged, entombed in their bony sepulchre for more than thirty centuries. When those ancient seeds were gathered up from the floor and placed in the ground they germinated and grew into a harvest of wheat, the same, and yet how different! The man of mechanical turn of mind takes in, without question, the ideas of his early teachers, forms, methods, words, and all, stores these goods away in the warehouse of his cranium, clamps down on them as bladder, vise and Egyptian skull did on their precious contents, and uses them unchanged all his life long, never using any others.

The slightest departure, not only from the old conceptions, but from the old and well-worn phraseology, is looked upon with grave suspicion, if not with apprehension of peril for the cause. The vital understanding sits at the feet of the same teachers, feeds on the same pabulum, takes in the same conceptions of truth and righteousness, but they root themselves in his mind, they enter into his consciousness, they hook themselves to the law of evolution and he begins to grow, and the products of this growth in life and character are a part of himself, they are instinct with life and power, they are not dead.

A mechanical theologian goes into the house of his soul, locks the doors, fastens the windows, draws the blinds, and thereby serves notice to the sun that no more light or ventilation is wanted or needed in that house.

The Vital-Minded Religionist

The vital-minded religionist leaves the door unlocked, opens the windows, puts up the blinds, and says all the air and light I can get in here is welcome on these premises. Our reformatory cause has had conspicuous instances of these types, and many variations of them, in its educators and ministers. Two cases of these temperamental differences have already been marked in the personalities of Isaac Errett and Moses E. Lard. Two others as widely differentiated in type, Dr. Winthrop H. Hopson and George W. Longan, are to be the subjects of our present study; to be followed by a paper on John W.McGarvey and Alexander Procter, almost extreme examples of the types of which I have been speaking.

My sole object in grouping our teaching around the personality of its historic leaders is to give it interest and verisimilitude. Personality is the finality of God's creation, and it is pretty much the only thing in which humanity has any vital concern. The great Joseph Parker once remarked, when he had read a book on theology he hastened to the story of the prodigal son, to take the bad taste out of his mouth. This masterpiece of our Lord's parables had as much theology in it as any page of the other book on Systematic Divinity. It had also thinking, feeling, acting, talking, personality in it, and that wins any day against the discussion of abstract propositions. These biographical touches are added only to make the discussion vital and of human interest.

DR. WINTHROP H. HOPSON

Dr. Hopson, to speak of him first, was a great preacher, a magnetic speaker, a man of attractive and commanding appearance in the pulpit. His thought was virile and clear, his language affluent and copious, his voice was mellow and agreeable, and his power to make himself felt and understood was remarkable. As a sermon architect and builder he had no equal among the Disciples, who were rich in great preachers of sermons. His powers of generalization, classification, and logical arrangement were far beyond the ordinary. In fact, his ideals of sermonic perfection were such that he sometimes sacrificed accuracy of statement to harmonious arrangement in his sermon outlines. His celebrated sermon of "The Three-fold Aspects of Divine Truth" is a good instance of this homiletic peculiarity of the Doctor and will also serve as an illustration of his conception of the way of salvation, a theme on which the Disciples of his time were particularly strong.

"Three-fold Aspects of Divine Truth"

I heard him preach this sermon twice, and according to my watch, it took him two hours and thirty minutes each time to deliver it. He occupied the first hour in gathering up and marshaling in solid array the sacred threes of the Bible. Three persons in the trinity; Father, Son, and Holy Spirit; three kingdoms, nature, grace and glory; three dispensations of religion, patriarchal, Jewish and Christian; three crowns, the crown of life, the crown of righteousness and the crown of glory; three conditions of salvation, faith, repentance and baptism, and so on, I forget how many triads there were.

This proposition was followed by one still more elaborate, in which it was affirmed that these trinities were all climactic. In every instance the third member was the consummation and, therefore, of more fundamental importance than either of the other two. The Holy Spirit being the last of the Godhead to participate in the work of human redemption, the culminating agency in the divine process of salvation was of more importance than the Father or the Son. The Christian dispensation, the sunlight age of revelation, being last and immeasurably the greatest, was more important than the starlight and moonlight economies of patriarchs and Jews. It was a self-evident statement of truth that the crown of glory exceeded in brilliancy and greatness the crowns of life and righteousness. By the time he had reached this point, and perhaps before, even as a callow youth in my teens, I began to see a breaker ahead, I waxed a little nervous and wondered if the great Doctor, with all his ingenuity in making things fit, and his dogmatic boldness, would march up to his logic, and face the music when he came to baptism! Well, he did. Without a quiver or a tremor of hesitation or trepidation, he marched boldly up, affirming flatfootedly that baptism as the consummating act of obedience in the process of salvation, and the point where the blessing of pardon and peace was first realized, was of commanding importance, even beyond that of faith and repentance. It goes without saying, that a man of Dr. Hopson's intellect and spiritual vision did not really believe that immersion in water as a religious ordinance was of more importance than faith and repentance. The eloquent Doctor was engaged in the exceedingly important business of saving his climaxes and the logical harmonies of his sermon.

A Tripartite Joke

This tripartite discourse, owing to circumstances that grew out of its delivery, became quite famous, if not historic, in the preacherhood of the Restoration. It is related that he held a protracted meeting at Eminence, Ky., during the pastorate of Sam Kelley, a well-known preacher and debater of the time, a man with a saving sense of wit and humor. The great "three" sermon had been delivered on Sunday morning, and as a group of brethren made their way homeward in company with the preachers, about two o'clock in the afternoon, where much fried chicken had long been waiting for consumption by the belated and hungry saints, the Doctor said to the pastor: "Brother Sam, what did you think of my sermon this morning?"

"Fine, Doctor, exceedingly fine."

"Was it not logical, scriptural and conclusive?" queried the preacher.

"Yes," replied the pastor, "it was unmistakably logical, scriptural and conclusive, but," he added, "it was not quite exhaustive."

"How is that?" said the preacher, surprised at the intimation that he could have failed to exhaust anything in sight that morning.

"You left out an important trinity," continued the humorous pastor.

"Pray, what could that have been?" said the astonished Doctor.

"Breakfast, dinner and supper," answered Bro. Sam.

The great shout of laughter that broke the stillness of the Sunday air showed that the point had gone home.

The Hopson "Bible College"

The big preachers of that day moulded the bullets for the little ones to fire. The young theologues and preachers of the ancient order were so eager to learn from the masters they would ride long distances, under all kinds of difficulties, sometimes on horseback, and sometimes on "the ankle bone express," to hear the big preachers preach their big sermons. They would sit for hours, spellbound, listening to these master of assemblies, and it was marvelous what a vast quantity of predigested theological material they could take in. Nothing escaped them, facts, arguments, allusions, illustrations, unconsidered trifles like pulpit mannerisms, were absorbed into their mental systems like water into a sponge. This was their Bible college, their theological seminary, and it wasn't a bad one, either. Dr. Hopson had such an easy facility in the construction of analyses and outlines, such fluency and grace in arranging and marshaling his propositions, that he became a great favorite to learn from and repeat after. This "three" sermon, to which I have been referring, was preached by scores of men all over the country, and sometimes with as much effect and power as the original.

In fact, "The Three Aspects of Divine Truth" became so prevalent in action and repetition, that it got on the nerves of some of the brethren to such an extent that Thomas Munnell, one of the ablest and most spiritual writers of the period, felt called upon to puncture it in an ironical article published in *Lard's Quarterly*. In the spirit of melodrama and mock heroics, Bro. Munnell ransacked the heavens above, the earth beneath, and the water under the earth. Metaphorically, he beat the bush in all the realms and spheres of the universe where triplets of any kind or description were likely to be found. Where the sacred number seven abounded threes, sacred and otherwise, did much more abound. These were dragged out from their hiding places and marshaled across the pages of the Quarterly in stately and scientific order. It was then observed with great solemnity and impressive dignity that these trinities were all culminating and climactic, including breakfast, dinner and supper ; that is to say, the third and last represents the ascending scale, and is therefore of more fundamental value than the other two members that precede it and lead up to it. That, said he, is the reason that baptism is more important than faith and repentance. Thus reductio ad absurdum put an end to the abuse connected with the plagiarism of the "Three-fold Aspect of Divine Truth.'' It was a great sermon preached by a great preacher, who was not to blame for other people abusing their privileges over much.

Proclamation of First Principles

Dr. Hopson's great ability as a preacher was seen to best advantage in his proclamation of "First Principles." He doted on the "everlasting yea" of faith, repentance and baptism, the remission of sins, the gift of the Holy Spirit, and certain of the fundamental characteristics of the apostolic church. The "blessed dogmatism" of the gospel, in its elements, appealed vigorously to the Doctor's imagination. As an exterminator of sects and sectarianism, he was a man of "'immense magnitude and huge ponderosity." He went straight and hard for the solar plexus of all opposition to the restoration cause. How he filled us Disciples with an uncontrollable enthusiasm in those good old days, when he landed square onto the fifth rib of sectarian opponents and denominational advocates, tumbling them over the ropes, always to be counted out, when— we did the counting. When he preached on the "Plan of Salvation" or "The Scheme of Redemption," his critics ungraciously said it was all plan and no salvation; mostly scheme and precious little redemption; and while this was partly true, it was by no means all true. All of the churches fifty years ago, more or less, conceived of the gospel in terms of legalism, they spoke of the kingdom of God in terms of politics and geography. It was kingdom, king, subjects, territory, laws, constitution, conditions of citizenship, naturalization of aliens, oath of allegiance to the government; all to be literally and legalistically construed. In an age when men fight each other with texts of Scripture, they are necessarily concerned with the letter of those text weapons, the spirit must be left to do the best it can for itself. It is a blessed thing, however, that under the most rigid and legalistic construction of the gospel, enough spiritual light gets in to convert sinners, and make saints of believers. The theology of the situation is a little wrong in the head, but the religion is all right in the heart.

Surprise Power of Great Orators

Dr. Hopson had the surprise power of great orators. Sometimes he would startle his hearers by the enunciation of a proposition which was so palpably literalistic and juridic as to be a plain violation of the spirit of the gospel and the mind of Christ. A typical instance is found in his sermon in the "Living Pulpit of the Christian Church," on "Baptism Essential to Salvation." After offending a part of his audience, and frightening all of them by the bald statement that his theme was, "Baptism Essential to Salvation," be would pause for a moment, square himself in the pulpit, shrug his shoulders, first one and then the other, and then commence with great deliberation and perfect composure: "Will a man, then, he damned if he is not baptized? Certainly, why not?" If the hearers could get consent of prejudice to listen carefully for awhile to the explanation that followed this sensational announcement, they generally found themselves in substantial harmony with the speaker.

As heterodox as he seemed to be in sound, he was practically orthodox in sense.

Assertion was followed by interpretation, which made it plain that the eloquent preacher did not for a moment believe that the physical act of immersion in water, either within itself considered, or in relation to any of its associations as an ordinance, was literally necessary to the salvation of the soul. From the point of view of this particular sermon, baptism was regarded as faith and repentance out of doors; as faith and repentance in action and manifestation; faith and repentance objectified and made into a visible and tangible line of demarcation between Christ and the world; the outer sign of God's inner covenant with the soul, and, hence, an act of obedience, involving the authority of Christ, and submission to him as Lord of all. A man who would reject or neglect a baptism like this could hardly expect salvation by the gospel as the New Testament records it.

While this sermon and many others preached by Dr. Hopson were pitched to the key of the legalistic and dogmatic in religion, a deeper insight and a broader vision appeared now and again, sufficient to make it plain that he had enough of the vital in his mental composition to insure a continuous growth to the end. Like Lard, his horizon broadened and brightened towards the going down of the sun. The charity, catholicity and spirituality of the gospel he had so often preached and vindicated, became more real to him in life as the days of the years of his pilgrimage were lengthened out. Always kind-hearted, generous and manly, he did a great work for God and humanity in his time, stood high in the love and esteem of his brethren. He died in the faith of the church of all good people.

GEORGE W. LONGAN

Geo. W. Longan, of Missouri, as philosophical thinker, profound reasoner, and luminous expositor of the Bible and the Christian religion, has had no superior among the Disciples in the three generations of their history. As theologian and literary exponent and interpreter of a spiritual religion, it is doubtful if he had an equal, who committed his thoughts to paper. His excessive modesty, his lack of ambition and self-assertion, put a serious limit on the area of his activity and influence. Not that he was like the "full many a flower," of Gray's Elegy, "born to blush unseen and waste its sweetness on the desert air," still one cannot help regretting that one so capable of molding thought and inspiring life should have failed of an adequate opportunity to fulfill his high commission. Only a few of the most thoughtful, who least needed his help, found access to the treasures of his thought, and the striking literary form in which it found expression. As an essayist he was great; greater in the opinion of the writer than any of his contemporaries. His articles published in the Quarterlies were masterpieces of theological exposition, and no one needed to hasten from them to something lighter to take the bad taste out of his mouth, unless the mouth in question held the palate of a trash-doped feather-head or a fish-brained ignoramus. His book in reply to Whittset's on "Mormonism the Offspring of Campbellism," little known to the brotherhood, probably out of print, is a meritorious performance, especially as a constructive statement of restoration principles.

Trend of His Sermonology

Mr. Longan's sermon in the "Living Pulpit" is one of the finest in the book, both as theology and as literature. It treats of the same theme as Dr. Hopson's, but notice the characteristic difference in statement of topic and treatment of theme; "Baptism Essential to Salvation," "The Conditions of the Gospel Reasonable."

If Phillips Brooks was right when he said, "No preaching ever had any strong power that was not the preaching of doctrine," these sermons had "strong power," and so had all the rest of that day. Both of these strong men were doctrinal preachers, but their intellectual concepts in the field of doctrine were not always the same. They interpreted Christianity as the religion of authority, but they did not ground authority in the same place. Hopson based the doctrine of baptism for the remission of sins on the literal warrant of Scripture. The amnesty proclamation of a king to a world in rebellion against its ruler. Longan found the relation of baptism to salvation in the moral significance of the ordinance, in the truth which it embodied and represented. Hopson found his explanation in the old distinction between positive and moral law, at one time a great favorite among the Disciples. Positive law was right because it was commanded, moral law was commanded because it was right. Ordinances like baptism were backed up by divine appointment and command, and this was the sole reason why they should be observed. In fact, it was held that obedience to positive law was a finer test of loyalty than obedience to moral law, for most anybody will obey a law the reason of which he can see; only men of strong faith and devotion will submit to a law for which there is no reason or righteousness, except that God has commanded it. We were fond of arbitrary divine appointment in those days, because we entertained the funny notion that God had the right to do things just because he could.

Bro. Longan denied that there was any such distinction in the spiritual realm as that between positive and moral law. No command, either human or divine, can change the nature of moral issues. Everything that God commands is right in itself or God would not command it. Whether we can or can not discern the reason of a divine precept, the reason is there, and that much, at least, if necessary, we may take by faith. The philosophical necessity, intrinsic reasonableness, and plain common sense, of faith and repentance, as terms and means of salvation, it was easy enough to demonstrate to people of ordinary intelligence; but how could baptism in any relation to remission of sins, be justified in the category of moral law, where things are commanded because they are right and necessary in themselves? If baptism were immersion only or chiefly this could not be done. The best effort that had been made up to 1868, among the Disciples, to penetrate the psychological and spiritual meaning of the ordinance, is found in this sermon on "The Conditions of the Gospel Reasonable."

"Conditions of the Gospel Reasonable"

This somewhat lengthy extract, justified under the circumstances, will make that fact appear:

"In all the universe, the penitent sinner's status, until developed in an overt act, is known only to himself and to God. But he has sinned openly. With a bold front he has measured arms with Omnipotence. His rebellion has not been confined to his heart. It has not exhausted itself in sympathy. Men on earth, the partners of his crime, have been the witnesses, and angels in heaven have looked on with astonishment at his defiant airs. Now, what does the nature of the case seem to demand? Where does it appear to be proper that

God should meet this once bold and defiant, but now humble and stricken outlaw? Where should God require him to stand, when he bestows upon him the boon of a merciful forgiveness of all his past sins? I answer, 'Out before heaven and earth, confessing his guilt, avowing his repentance, and pledging himself to unflinching fidelity in all time to come.' His faith and repentance must be embodied in an overt act, that men and angels can see. Surely this is clear beyond cavil. Sinner, in this issue between God and Satan, your rightful lawgiver demands that you shall define your position. He requires you to choose whom you will serve, and to declare your choice before heaven and earth. Are you for your rightful sovereign, or do you stand in the ranks of the enemy? God has established an institution and made it the line of separation between his kingdom and that of the opposing power. This institution is Christian baptism. In this overt act you externalize your faith and repentance, and make them visible to your fellow-men. In this act you formally and solemnly dedicate yourself to God. In it, you vow eternal allegiance to His throne. In it, all the holy desires and heaven-born resolves of the inner man take upon them an outward form, and can be seen and read by your associates. Is it strange that God should demand such an expression of your faith in Him? Such a pledge of eternal fealty in time to come? Nay, it would have been strange, indeed, if God had tendered forgiveness without it. It has its foundation in the eternal fitness of things. Its reason is clear as a sunbeam. It is not the value of the thing done. It is not that it has saving merit in it. It is not that water, as such, has power to cleanse from guilt. Baptism is no charm. It has in it no mystery. Its sole value is this: That as an open public avowal of your faith and penitence, as a formal and solemn dedication of yourself to God, in a heaven-appointed way, it places you in a proper position before heaven and earth to receive the free and gracious forgiveness of your past sins."

His Mind Grew with His Years

Forty-six years ago this was the best possible interpretation of the psychology of baptism in New Testament evangelism. G.W. Longan being an intensely vital man did not stop growing at the age of forty-nine. He lived thirty years longer and, like Gladstone, he grew to the last day. That stage of brain petrifaction called the dead line he never crossed. A subsequent revision of this exposition of the philosophy of baptism for the remission of sins, while not subtracting anything from what had been written, would have added elements of greater depth as to the philosophical and real significance of baptism in its relation to salvation of the soul. As to this we will see farther on in these reflections. Geo. W. Longan was one of the first of Disciple leaders to face modern issues from the point of view of the modem mind. Instead of receding from him as a back number, it will be a long time before we reach the "everlasting yea" for which he stood.

JOHN W. MCGARVEY AND ALEXANDER PROCTER

*Two Representatives of
Conservative and Progressive Leadership*

JOHN W. MCGARVEY

As President McGarvey was my teacher in the old Bible College of Kentucky University and a life-long friend and helper, I must pay the first tribute of esteem and affection to him, as a great and most influential factor in the making of Disciple history.

When I entered the college in the fall of 1869, he was in his forty-first year, but looked much younger. He looked boyish, but no one, after hearing him, made the mistake of taking him for a boy. While less magnetic and commanding in personality when compared to some of the men of whom I have written, in the fulness and clearness of his knowledge of the Book of books and his ability to communicate it in simple and vital English, he was not equalled by any of them. He was past master of facts and texts.

He had acquired more historical and textual knowledge of Holy Scriptures than any man of his time. One of his eastern guides spoke of him as "that little man from Kentucky who measured every hole in Palestine with a tape-line"; but he knew as much of the geography and topography of the Holy Land before his visit as he did after. His mastery of the land and the book has hardly been equalled in our time. One of the most impressive characteristics of his knowledge was its unfailing accuracy. In the matter of historical information concerning facts or texts, it was the rarest thing in the world that he was ever known to make a mistake. An opponent must make sure of his facts before he dared to measure arms with this little man from Kentucky.

His Prodigious Industry

The simplicity and clearness with which he imparted knowledge was equally remarkable. No man ever used words with a stricter reference to their meaning. Like the apostle Paul, he used "great plainness of speech," so much so that a child could follow, and grown people wondered if anybody couldn't talk like that. This, however, was the art that concealed art. So great was the simplicity of his sermons and addresses that a stream of light was left behind in which the humblest of his hearers could walk. Like John Wesley he was methodical and regular in his habits. His industry was prodigious, although to the onlooker its prodigiousness was not apparent. He worked with such ease, and with such absence of noise and friction, that he did not seem to be working at all. If at any time his place had been vacant, it would have taken two first-class men to continue his work. He had four classes in college and lectured four times a day. He contributed regularly, most of the time, to two or three of our periodicals. He had a very large correspondence, asking all kinds of questions on all kinds of subjects. Every letter was answered with his own hand. He had frequent calls for lectures and speeches; was pastor of the Broadway Christian Church several years, and of three other churches, with as much preaching and pastoral work as other men had, with nothing else to do; he had always one book, and sometimes two or three, in process of preparation, besides matters of family interest and business that always take a considerable slice out of a man's time. In addition to this long list of strenuous labors, all of his numerous books and literary contributions to magazines and papers were written in odd hours between classes and at home in the evening between the hours of eight and ten. In addition to his voluminous writings he gave more oral instruction than any man among the Disciples.

McGarvey on Acts

His first book, written when he was about thirty-five, a commentary on the Acts of the Apostles, was perhaps his most notable achievement in the art of book production. The peculiarity of this work was the originality of the form of comment and exposition, which the author was one of the first to adopt. Commentaries before this time had been like the old woman's dictionary, "Mighty interestin' readin', but powerful disconnected and scatterin'" Instead of exegetical comment on single texts, one after the other, the new style was continuous, historical exposition, that one could take up and read through like a book of history or a work of fiction. This was the first book of the kind I had read through and the last, until thirty-five years later, I began to read the "Expositors' Bible Series," and George Adam Smith's two books on Isaiah. McGarvey's Commentary on Acts is still bought and read, and no better manual of Disciple teaching on the first principles of the Gospel has yet been written.

Simplicity of Teaching

His method of teaching his classes was simplicity and perspicacity in the most effective style of the art. He taught the historical books of both Testaments, touching prophetic books and apostolic epistles only when they were in some way related to the history. He analyzed the narratives of these historical books, according to their subject matter, into divisions, sections, paragraphs, notes and queries. He wrote these down, and gave them out in his lecture, for the next day's recitation. He did not aim at verbal accuracy or completeness in reciting Old Testament lessons; he gave the sense in his own words, requiring only the same of the student. In later years he put these analyses on the blackboard, leaving students to copy them at their leisure. Later still, when they had been changed and perfected, they were printed and distributed for the use of his classes. In each recitation the students were required to reproduce the lecture of the previous day. In my day we committed the New Testament histories verbatim, and for good count gave back to the Professor every point of his last lecture. When we had finished Sophomore and Junior under "Little Mac," as we called him, we knew Matthew, Mark, Luke and John, and the Acts of the Apostles by heart, and we knew the historical books of the Old Testament in pretty much the same way. This thorough drill in the inspired Scriptures set us ten years forward in our studies and knowledge as ministers of the Gospel. That is to say, we were a decade in advance of anything we could have acquired by any efforts or methods of our own, or anything provided by the theological seminaries of that day or this.

The First Real Bible College

A Bible College where the Bible is the textbook, to be directly studied and taught, was the conception of Prof. McGarvey and its establishment the greatest achievement of his life. This institution was for a long time the only real Bible College in the world; a Theological Seminary is a different affair. It was a veritable modern school of the prophets, and by means of it and the holy passion with which he expounded the truths of the book, he became the molder and maker of more preachers than any other man of his day.

His Devotion to the Word of God

One of the things that most distinguished this man of God was his supreme devotion to the Bible as the word of God. He loved the book as few men loved it. In his ordination vows he took out a brief to defend the Bible through thick and thin; no matter how thick, and no matter how thin. Like a scribe of the ancient law, he was a legal advocate who vindicated his client at all hazards, and against all odds. His resources, skill and ingenuity as an ecclesiastical lawyer were magnificent, and also, war. He maintained from first to last the theory of the verbal inspiration and absolute inerrancy of the Scriptures. He knew nothing of a human element in the Bible unless it was closely guarded and censored by the divine. The first chapters of Genesis were not religious poems to reveal God, but a scientific manual to make known the order and succession of the different elements of the creation. The Mosaic cosmogony was literal fact or literal falsehood. He knew history and its lessons, but nothing of the idealization of history for teaching purposes. Bible writers were men of literary genius, but unlike all other great writers of their time, and all time, in the literary framework of Biblical statements and stories, the creative imagination was never brought into use. They never condescended to idealize their material, or to employ tradition, fiction, myth, or legend, for didactic or illustrative ends. Brother McGarvey went the length of denying that there was an element of fiction, or work of the imagination, in the parables of Jesus. The stories of the Rich Man and Lazarus and the Prodigal Son were based on observation of facts, not fancy.

No Room for Imagination

Isaiah was Isaiah, Daniel was Daniel, Job was Job, Jonah in particular was Jonah, the great fish and all, and Baalam's ass spake as good Hebrew as his master, and what else? This great teacher of history and fact, doctrine and the letter of Scripture, did not neglect the spirit, which he possessed in large measure, and taught to others; but he was deficient in the kind of a temperament suited to a profound and adequate interpretation of an Oriental book abounding, as it does on almost every page, with figures of speech, imagery, poetry and symbolism.

My old teacher hadn't enough imagination or glow of feeling for a pulpit orator, but his preaching was unique and wonderfully interesting and instructive. From the point of view of sermon construction and illustration, peculiarly his own, and yet most effective, I have never heard anyone preach as he did. His method was original and has not, to my knowledge, been successfully copied by anyone else. He would select a text from the New Testament, for instance, from which he would educe a single truth or principle; and then, instead of the anecdotal and personal illustrations of other preachers, he would take up an Old Testament story, bearing on his theme, which he would relate and revitalize in all of its most striking details, clinching points, and bringing out lessons, as he proceeded to his main conclusion. I heard him preach from a New Testament text on jealousy which he amplified and illustrated by telling the story of Saul's persecution of David. This narrative told in a simple, artless, and almost dramatic manner, was the main body of his sermon, illustrating by a concrete instance the wickedness and futility of the green-eyed monster.

Those who said there was no religion in the book of Esther because the name of God is not found in it, should have heard the professor preach on the special providence of God over his people, demonstrating and illustrating his theme by the simple narration of the story of Esther, in which he showed that God and the power of God for the deliverance of those who trust in Him, were in every verse; the only thing missing was the number of letters, rightly assembled, it took to spell his name. He always claimed that this method of preaching had two advantages, first, it illustrated his subject, and second, it familiarized the minds of his hearers with the Word of God.

His Doctrinal Preaching

As a doctrinal preacher, his style of sermonizing was somewhat different. I once heard him through a protracted meeting preach a series of sermons on the cases of conversion in the Acts of Apostles. If anyone in that community failed to catch the New Testament idea of conversion it was not the fault of the preacher to whom they had been listening. The Lexington Professor "lightened" in those sermons, and General R.M. Gano came along soon after and "thundered" and a great harvest of souls was gathered into the kingdom. Those were days of doctrinal preaching, followed by emotional exhortations.

It was on what the Disciples called the elements of the gospel or first principles that they differed the most radically from their religious neighbors. On these elemental features of the message, faith, repentance, baptism, remission of sins, the gift of the Holy Spirit, as conditions of salvation and church membership, the subject of this sketch was particularly strong, and in his earlier day somewhat combative.

A suggestive instance may be cited here of an episode that occurred in Lexington in 1870 or 1871. When the big congregation in the old Main Street Church overflowed and swarmed, and the new hive had been temporarily settled in the opera house, the new organization purchased the old brick Presbyterian Church on Broadway. Prof. McGarvey, who had been installed as pastor of the new congregation, a few days before they were to take possession, remarked half facetiously to a friend, that he proposed on the day of entrance and dedication to deliver the first gospel sermon ever preached in that house. This half jocular threat was incautiously repeated, and the fat was in the fire. The "sects" of that day took their cue from Ishmael, and the whole denominational outfit was a unit in peculiar manifestations of displeasure against the Disciples. James Lane Allen's "Reign of Law" picture of the theological situation in the capital of the Blue Grass region in the late 60's and early 70's, while technically inaccurate in a few particulars, was substantially correct, both in spirit and in truth. The Bible College Professor was denounced for his narrowness and bigotry, and as many bitter things were said as the occasion seemed to call for. "Little Mac" was not a man to back down in the face of a hostile demonstration. He straightened himself up, and putting a little more stiffening material into his vertebra to bear the added burden of obloquy to be heaped upon him, he said, "I made that remark in a joke, but since they have made so much fuss about it, I will make it good. I will preach next Sunday night on 'What is a Gospel Sermon?' and I will demonstrate the literal correctness of my assertion."

Definition of a Gospel Sermon

The first point was a gospel sermon in outline according to the Calvinistic theology of current Presbyterianism.

1. Original sin and hereditary total depravity.
2. Unconditional election and reprobation.
3. Special grace and particular redemption.
4. Miraculous regeneration by the Holy Spirit.
5. Remission of sins.
6. Repentance.
7. Faith.
8. Baptism by affusion.
9. Church membership.

Then began the outline of a gospel sermon as he and his brethren understood the gospel.

1. Jesus of Nazareth the Son of God, so demonstrated by his resurrection, ascension and coronation as Divine Savior and universal Lord.
2. Personal faith in the personal Christ, based on the Divine testimony concerning Him.
3. Repentance, a change of the will toward God and righteousness.
4. Baptism in the name and by the authority of Christ.
5. Remission of sins.
6. The gift of the Holy Spirit.
7. Spiritual fellowship and church membership.

Here are two sermons, widely different, claiming to represent the gospel according to the New Testament, which one, if either, is correct? It is no use to compare the one with the other, for that would be to run in a circle and beg the question at issue. If a standard can be found, the authority and sufficiency of which are admitted by both parties to the dispute, the test can be easily applied and the question settled. He brought in the old yard-stick illustration at this point. If the yard-sticks of two merchants did not agree in length, the legality of these measuring instruments could only be determined by taking them to the court-house, and comparing them with the infallible yard-stick kept on hand for settling such disputes as this. Here are two theological yard-sticks, not of the same length, obviously one or the other, and possibly both, are wrong, shall we exhibit as much grace and common sense as those hypothetical merchants who made comparison with a measuring instrument admittedly correct and thus forever brought their controversy to an end?

Peter at Pentecost the Test

Fortunately for us we have only to carry our sermonic yard-sticks over to the court house of the Temple in Jerusalem and lay them alongside the one used by the inspired Peter on the day of Pentecost, and the dispute is settled, and because settled right is settled forever. He laid down the Presbyterian sermon and it did not "subtend the analogy of the case" at a single point. Even where gospel elements were put in they were vitiated and disintegrated, being put in the wrong place. When the professor laid his own sermon down by the side of the infallible standard, chosen by common consent as the ideal of comparison, it fit all round to the queen's taste. Indeed, it was not the professor's outline at all, it was an analysis of Peter's sermon itself, which converted three thousand souls on the occasion of its first delivery. The Disciples were jubilant, the Presbyterians silent. Our Calvinistic brethren were squelched, in about the same way, I suppose, that Brother McGarvey was when J.B. Briney unhorsed him on the organ question, for, a man convinced against his will is of the same opinion still.

To Mr. Briney belong the honors of killing the organ conscience in Kentucky, by the complete overthrow of its father and first champion in a public discussion pulled off in the pages of the *Apostolic Times* forty years ago; and also of shattering the firm belief of his students that their favorite professor was invincible in debate —and so he was, unless he had the weak side and a strong opponent, and he certainly had both in that historic tussle on the organ question.

Mr. McGarvey's Firmness and Conservatism

Brother McGarvey was firm and, under provocation, obstinate. He was one of the immutables who never changed. When he put his foot down it was down. When once a conviction was formed in his mind, an opinion espoused, or a cause championed, he remained with it without change to the end. And yet he did not entirely escape the law of evolution and the process of the suns. He was never converted to the organ, but he ceased openly to oppose it. The polemic and combative attitude of his work in the earlier years was softened and modified as time went on, except when he was chasing a higher critic. No one that knew him will controvert the statement that he was entirely conscientious in the belief that it was his sacred duty and solemn responsibility to stand between his brethren and all danger from what he called "destructive criticism." He was a conservative of conservatives temperamentally, and hence the slightest change was unwarranted and dangerous innovation. He always had the courage of his convictions, was always on the firing line, fighting for what he believed to be the truth of God. His critical column in the *Christian Standard*, which he conducted for about twenty years, though able, and at times thorough, did not add anything to his reputation as scholar or theologian. The spirit of ridicule, banter, and sarcasm so often took the place of serious argument on the merits of the issue that quite as much harm as good was done. To be always plastering the blisters onto the unprotected skin of your opponent does the plasterer harm and the plastered no good. People who had no personal knowledge of Professor McGarvey, who had to form their opinion of him from his critical and controversial writing, had no true conception of the real man. When they conceived of him as cross, crabbed, and picayunish, they were shooting through an old abandoned suit of clothes hung up to scare the crows. The man had stepped out and was generally engaged in better business than scaring crows; although from his point of view, this was a duty that had to be performed and not with any special reference to the feelings of these black-suited, destructive critics who were pulling up the young corn in the field of the Lord. A kinder-hearted, sweeter-spirited man, one more devoted to the highest ideals of divine service and human living, it would have been hard to find.

He once read me out of the synagogue for a pronouncement of mine on the subject of Biblical criticism, but he did it in such manifest pain and sorrow, and with such expressions of esteem and appreciation, that there was nothing to forgive on my part, and no interruption of the friendly relations that had always existed between us. I did not always agree with him, but I loved him all the same.

ALEXANDER PROCTER

In this writing of John William McGarvey and Alexander Procter I have not a scrap of data or source of information to draw from, only my personal knowledge and memory of the men. My long association and intimate acquaintance with the former has furnished me more material than I could use, but what shall be said of a king who never organized a court, sat on a visible throne, or left any record behind him? The hardest literary task is to write of a great man who lived only in his thoughts. If you undertake to reproduce his thinking, if he has written anything, your effort is superfluous, and worse than useless. If there are no events, episodes, outward happenings and idiosyncracies to hang points on, what are your Johnsons going to do, if they cannot find Boswells to snatch the great words from their tongues and put them down on paper, for the world's profit and edification?

"He Went about Saying Things"

Oh, what a loss it has been that the great man of Independence, Mo., never found his Boswell. He was a masterful talker, write he would not. This man of genius resembled his divine Master in more respects than one. W.T. Moore is credited with the observation that "Jesus did not preach but just went about sayin' things." This modern Disciple of the man of Nazareth did no mere conventional preaching, but if ever a teacher of men "just went about sayin' things," and great things, it was Alexander Procter. He would talk in his own wonderful and beautiful way to anybody, to individuals of no particular intelligence or importance, the same as to a philosopher, or a great crowd assembled to hear him preach. He had an aversion to writing even in private correspondence. I never heard of him answering a letter. Editors wrote him soliciting contributions for their papers, offering him liberal remuneration for his services, but these anxious communications were never answered, and no copy ever materialized. He did write one great piece on "Living Issues" for the *Christian Quarterly*, and a few fragments escaped his pen for early numbers of "The Christian," of which he was supposed to be one of the editors,

Poet, Philosopher, Saint

Like his Master, he spoke the simple word and launched the burning thought, leaving them to do their work in the hearts of men. He had no egotism and less dogmatism. Poet and philosopher and saint were combined in him in the right proportions to make a prophet. He was the second Isaiah of our spiritual reformation, the greatest of all the prophets our cause has yet produced. If the Lord intended to make a sectarian or a partisan of Alexander Procter, he put the wrong material in him for that purpose. He was positively too big of brain and large of soul to compress himself into the narrow limits of any sect or denomination extant. Logic-chopping, hair-splitting, Shibboleth-pronouncing, prejudice-engendering sectarianism, under no guise of pretense or sanctification, had any attraction for him. He once said to me, "I used to preach what a few believed and made sectarians, now I preach what everybody believes and make Christians." He cared little for the old orthodox distinctions of a formal theology; intellectual concepts of religion over which men quarrel did not interest him, unless they stood for the vital and the eternal in the Christian faith. His working creed was the absolute religion expressed by the two great commandments of the law and the prophets, the finalities of the faith represented by the mind of Jesus Christ. Spiritual insight, breadth of outlook, the open vision, a vital and ethical application of religious truth to the lives of men, and the healing of the wounds of Christendom, are the qualities that characterized his preaching, and his matchless talks were never so matchless as when Jesus Christ, his divine Savior and human brother, was the theme.

The mind of this universal man was a veritable "Cave of the Winds," into which blew breezes of thought and suggestion from every quarter, and his mind was open to every breeze.

Intellectually Receptive

He was intellectually hospitable to ideas, no matter from what direction they came, but he always maintained his virile intellectual independence and freedom. Things must be philosophically and rationally consistent and defensible to command his allegiance. Mere external authority in religion without reason, or justice, or necessity behind it did not weigh a feather with him. The only authoritative thing in the universe was truth, the only authoritative person Christ, and Christ was the incarnation of truth.

He had a mind that could penetrate essences and see into the nature of things, and was therefore never in the slightest degree influenced by minds that only hit the surface and saw into nothing. He had brains and spiritual vision to make the elements of a theology hang together, which other people were trying to save by hanging separately. I once heard him say that he did not believe in a personal devil, because there was no place for him in the universe of God. From the point of view of a Christian interpretation of the world, there was no place in a rational spiritual order for Theodore Parker's fourth person of the Trinity, or the Satanic Majesty of Milton's Paradise Lost. Like Henry Ward Beecher he was an early convert to the doctrine of evolution. He believed in the universality of the reign of law. He believed with Carlyle in a natural supernaturalism. From the viewpoint of the lawgiver, and the forces behind his laws, there was no suspension or violation of these laws in creation or in redemption, if we could rise to the comprehension of the higher levels. The same laws that operate in the stars and suns, in the continents and isles and oceans of the earth, operated in Palestine in the progressive development and evolution of the Christian religion, "One God, one law, one element, one far-off Divine event to which the whole creation moves."

Not Appreciated by Contemporaries

It goes without saying that a man of the dimensions of Alexander Procter was misunderstood, and only half appreciated by his religious contemporaries. It has always been so and it will be so for a long time to come. During our National Convention at Nashville, in 1892, a so-called religious paper of that city, which prides itself on being a representative of Jesus Christ and his mind of love, announced in its news columns that "the infidel Procter" from Missouri was present in the convention. The next day, in conversation, without referring to this item of intelligence to save the brotherhood from contamination, he said, "The most pathetic thing in the world is the fact that when a man comes to a view of God, Christ, and the Bible, which he can hold, and respect himself, from that moment he is denounced as a heretic and an infidel." I could not help but say, "Any worse, Brother Procter, than the same class of men said about the Master and all the prophets?" The fact of infinite pathos is, as long as the type of men who could speak of Alexander Procter as an infidel continue to edit religious newspapers and play the role of church leaders, both Christian union and the millennium will have to be indefinitely postponed.

A stenographer in his congregation, if I have been correctly informed, without the knowledge of the preacher, took down a number of his discourses, which have been published in the form of a volume of sermons. These selections contain many of the characteristic utterances of this Christ-inspired seer of the New Age. The glory of a cause is its great men. Judged by this standard the Disciple movement has had its share of glory. Many good and noble men, as these papers demonstrate, have plead this cause, but few of them have been as great, and none greater than the man Alexander Procter, who gave to our time the stimulus of a great appeal and the inspiration of a great example.

THE RESTORATION MOVEMENT UP TO DATE

A Christian minister delivered an able series of lectures in a western town on the great churches of Christendom, their founders, and respective missions in the historic evolution of Christianity. The peculiar characteristic of each and its distinctive contribution to religious development was pointed out, and in the closing part of each lecture, in addition to a summary of achievements, theological errors and doctrinal blunders were indicated as spots on the sun in the ecclesiastical and reformatory movements of history.

The Roman Catholic Church, the Greek Catholic, the Anglican, the Lutheran, the Presbyterian, the Congregational, the Methodist, Baptist, and Disciple, came under review, with their founders and representative leaders: Luther, Calvin, Henry the Eighth, Wesley, and the two Campbells. The serious mistakes of the older Protestant bodies and their efforts at reformation were the importations from Rome that hindered reform and multiplied sects. These doctrinal errors inherited from Romanism and passed along the line from one denomination to another, were specifically and plainly stated in each case, as still standing in the way of Christian union.

An intelligent lady in the congregation wondered to a neighbor, who sat by her side, if the lecturer would be as ready to uncover the doctrinal mistakes of his own religious body when the time came, as he had been in the case of all the others.

The speaker had no specifications in his indictment of doctrinal errors against the Disciples. He referred to the woman's remark but had drawn up no catalogue of theological mistakes against his brethren. He said very frankly that his own people were not infallible, they had never claimed to be, and he did not hesitate to affirm that few of the Disciples had realized their ideals, doctrinal or otherwise.

Is this arraignment quite as definite and specific as historical and theological accuracy require, in the issue raised by the lecturer's critic? Did the Disciples make no doctrinal mistakes in their passage from Protestant denominationalism which brought with it so many objectionable things from Rome? Have we failed to understand, and rightly to appraise the fact, that some of the denominations that had least of the doctrines of Rome had most of its spirit? Have we yet to learn that intellectual misconceptions, called erroneous doctrines, weigh as light as feathers in comparison with the spirit of pride, arrogance, intolerance, self-righteousness, and infallible cocksureness, generated by high church Phariseeism wherever you find it? The dogmatic interpretation of the Bible originated with Greek and Latin Christianity. Legalism and formalism came from the same source as far as Protestant churches are concerned. Protestantism was born in a rebellion against the dogmatics of Rome and Constantinople, and then in less than a generation set up a counter-irritant almost as bad; worse, in fact, in its emphasis of dogma, but not quite so rank in its stress of sacraments and priestcraft.

An Overplus of Intellectualism

The Disciples appear to have committed fewer doctrinal mistakes than their contemporaries, because they learned early in their history that there is no more salvation in a Protestant dogma than there is in a Roman Catholic ceremony. Their first weakness was an overplus of intellectualism. They conceived and interpreted religious truth in terms of the intellect, failing at first to perceive that this would lead them directly into the dogmatism and legalism from which they were trying to escape, and some of them have not perceived it yet, but most of them have. As the Disciples have been often charged with legalism and a legalistic construction of the law of the spirit of life in Christ Jesus, and I have used the term several times in these papers, it may be well to pause here and ask what the word connotes in our religious terminology, and how far they have been guilty of the charge which they have, with open-minded frankness, sometimes preferred against themselves.

Legalism stands to religion as technicality does to politics and the courthouse. It is the substitution of form for substance, letter for spirit, phraseology for fact, symbol for the thing symbolized. More correctly, perhaps, it is the exaltation of the form of godliness above the power, of the outward above the inward, the sign above the thing signified, intellectual belief above moral and spiritual character. The Quaker who when smitten on one cheek meekly turned the other and then said, "Now, friend, I have fulfilled the law, and I'll give thee a lickin'," was a legalist. In observing the letter he had broken the spirit. It was a conscientious and highly important act to keep the letter of the law, but of no importance whatever to keep the spirit. The man who insists on immersion more than on the regenerate life for which immersion stands, is legalistic, and guilty of exalting form above essence, and the letter above the spirit. Consciously the Disciples have never made this mistake in theory, but sometimes, unconsciously, they have made it in practice. The effort to abolish the distinction between the essential and the non-essential, the formal and the spiritual, and the assumption that the outward form is as indispensable as the inward meaning for which it stands, is one of the ear-marks of a legalistic construction of the Christian religion.

That the Disciples did make this mistake is abundantly attested by the preaching and the literature of the first two generations. The old distinction, so strenuously insisted on, between positive and moral law, and the belief that the truth was not obligatory till it became mandatory, were off the same piece of cloth. These things are seldom heard now, in either pulpit or press, except as relics of an almost forgotten past.

The Folly of Legalistic Religion

The worst thing in historic legalism is the assumption of finality and self-infallibility which inheres in all its conclusions. A typical legalist of the ancient order was an infallible man who never erred, and therefore an immutable man who never changed. All of his opinions were finalities. He had the truth, the whole truth, and nothing but the truth; other people must come to him or be damned. Some of us are still living who heard Dr. Hopson's famous saw, "Others may be right and they may be wrong, but we are right and can not be wrong." The man who suspends theological mountains by textual hairs, must be sure that his hairs will hold, and he always is. The creed of a new reform quickly crystallizes and assumes that the last word has been spoken. Its pillars of Hercules go up on the outer rim of things, with its encircling motto, Ne plus ultra—nothing beyond. This is petrifaction, and rocks are dead. There can be no Christian union with folks of this kind, for the other fellow must make all the concessions and do all the changing. A reformation of this type goes out on a mission of conquest, scalps dangle at its belt, as tokens of victory. Its only terms of union are those of General Grant in our Civil War: "Unconditional surrender."

As the Disciples were committed body and soul to the great cause of unification, on the foundation of Jesus Christ our Savior and Lord, they were bound to see in this assumption of finality in a human interpretation of the Scriptures, the consummation of all that was unintelligent and silly. They saw that flexibility was a fundamental characteristic of a working theology. If our fathers had left us an inflexible routine of perfect religious beliefs and practices, semper idem, like the Roman Catholic Church, we, their sons and daughters, would have nothing to do but to sit and look on. At best an inane and tiresome business! If God had made a perfect world at the start, with all loose ends fastened at both ends, all questions answered, all problems solved, all perfection of thought and life automatically attained, you and I, friend reader, would be out of a job, and the universe would be unspeakably a dull and dreary place in which to live. There is no finality in our religious conceptions, and there never will be, although it is the way of human nature, especially religious human nature, for each generation of men to take for granted that the heights of the absolute religion have been scaled, and no change beyond is thinkable. A pardonable conceit, perhaps, but regrettable on account of its consequences.

But the legalism of the early Disciple movement was inevitable if not justifiable. In the war with a wild emotionalism and a subtle mysticism, a literal, legal, and matter of fact construction of the constitution became a practical necessity. The man in the field and on the street is a born legalist. A plain, literal, common-sense proposition, backed up by clear, intelligible Scripture statements, that declare or confirm it, finds him, it hits where he lives, whereas, mystical and metaphysical references to the "inner light," and the baptism in Holy Ghost, which he has not experienced and does not understand, do not attract him. These legalistic expounders of the word made thousands of converts who had turned away from ecstatic emotionalism and mystic religionism as quite impossible to them. What they wanted was a plain gospel that could be proved by Scripture in a way that a plain man could understand it.

Moreover, a controversial age is necessarily a legalistic age. When men debate, they use the letter that kills, leaving the spirit that gives life to do the best it can for itself, under the circumstances. The polemic discusses words, phrases, forms, methods, and verbal propositions; spirituality and morality are not debatable questions. The Disciples came up in an age of dogmatism and disputation, and were therefore compelled to fight their way into recognition and success with such weapons as existing conditions put into their hands. The time for a hard and fast construction of our spiritual constitution to enforce the letter by compromising and sacrificing a large part of its spirit has passed; and the Disciples were a little slow at first to comprehend the change; of late years they have made rapid progress in the better way.

Some Outgrown Issues

The Disciples are no exception to the law of evolution. They have grown, and therefore they have changed, and they have changed continuously for the better. To say we had lived a century without growing would be equivalent to saying we had lived a hundred years without living, for to live is to grow and to grow is to change. In the world of intellectual construction, to live is to change, and to have lived long is to have changed often. As our fundamental aim is to realize the ideals of apostolic Christianity, the better we succeed the more marked and vital will be our changes, not so much in our conception as in our application of truth.

A man's theology is his explanation of religion in terms of the understanding, and hence theology is always in a state of flux, while religion remains the same. Changing attitudes of mind towards theological issues come about in two ways. First, these issues are settled or they pass into other and more vital issues; or second, they expire by statute of limitation and lack of breath. Most of the old questions that caused division and separation between Baptists and Disciples eighty years ago, like a Christian Scientist when he dies, have passed on. The famous sermon of Alexander Campbell on the Law, the chief cause of the rupture, and the war that followed would be innocuous and harmless, if preached today before the most provincial and out-of-date Baptist Association in America. The head and front of Mr. Campbell's offending was the affirmation that Christians are under the grace of Jesus Christ and not under the law of Moses, and everybody knows in these enlightened days that modern investigation has settled this question in favor of Mr. Campbell's contention and the Disciple position.

Forty years ago one of our favorite themes was "the setting up of the kingdom." We used the kingdom and the church as interchangeable terms, and we had no trouble in demonstrating the proposition that the kingdom was "set up" and the church established on the first Pentecost after the resurrection. Our Baptist brethren affirmed that the church began in the wilderness of Judea under the ministry of John the Baptist, and some of them thought that was the reason the Baptist church was called Baptist. This is another one of the old issues that modern scholarship has completely settled in favor of the Disciples.

The ancient controversy on the priority of faith or repentance died a natural death because there was not enough in it to keep it alive. After debating several decades on the unpsychological question as to whether faith came before repentance or repentance before faith, they woke one morning with clear heads from a long night's sleep, to discover that their discussion had been pure logomachy—a war of words. They saw at once, according to the constitution of the human mind and the will of God, if a man believes and repents at all he must believe and repent in the right way, that an unbeliever cannot repent, and an impenitent man cannot trust, and therefore there must be two elements in faith, one before repentance and the other after, so that both parties had been right in what they affirmed and wrong in what they denied, as is usually the case with people who debate religious questions.

Some years ago when engaged in conversation with a young Baptist pastor in a Southern city, a graduate of one of their leading colleges and theological seminaries, something was said of the old, out-worn issue between Baptists and Disciples, about as they have been stated here, when the young man innocently said, "And which side did the Baptists take?" This was immensely funny to one of the parties to that conversation, but perhaps some of our own sprouting theologues are similarly well informed on the dead issues of a generation ago, which are not even taught as history in our denominational schools.

Our Growth in Spirituality

The Disciples have grown, almost from the beginning, in the matter of their attitude towards the Holy Spirit. The old charge that they denied the Holy Spirit never had any semblance of truth in it. They believed profoundly and reverently all that the Bible said on the subject, but they questioned many things affirmed by ignorance and superstitious fanaticism, and the frothy emotionalism of the time. As one extreme usually begets another, it was rather to be expected that some of the early teachers would enter the speculative realm, and unduly rationalize the work of the Spirit. A negligible number believed that the word of God and the Holy Spirit were one and the same. There was a general disposition to admit his personality as the third person in the Trinity, but some of the brethren made no other use of him than to inspire the Bible and reveal the plan of salvation. In itemizing and elucidating the gospel for the benefit of inquiring sinners, the gift of the Spirit was put in as number five; being the mystical element in the process, however, they felt that they did not certainly understand, and it was really inserted in the interest of theory and classification because Peter put it in on the day of Pentecost. They were faithful in following the Bible even when they were not certain that they understood where it would lead them. The current interpretation of the baptism in the Holy Spirit, to be administered by the Savior, as the distinguishing characteristic of his reign, made it out a miraculous affair to launch the new dispensation confined to the twelve apostles, or at most, to the hundred and twenty disciples present when the gospel was first preached and the church established.

A correspondent wrote to Professor McGarvey asking, "Why, in all your voluminous writings have you had so little to say on the subject of the Holy Spirit?" He answered with commendable frankness: "Because I know so little about it." That same professor knew more of the Bible than anybody, and the book from beginning to end is full of the Holy Spirit. His sermon in the Living Pulpit is based on a great Pauline mysticism: "The Spirit himself bears witness with our spirit that we are the children of God," but he rationalized it by an effort to show that the Spirit bears witness through the Word. The late David King of England said in an annual conference of the Old Disciples: "The Holy Spirit is in the church, but not in its individual members." "Yes," answered a spiritual man, speaking from the floor of the house, "that is like saying: there is life in the forest but none in the trees, life in the army but none in the soldiers."

When Isaac Errett said, in his Detroit "Synopsis," "The Spirit that indicts the Word can best bring home to the heart the significance of its truth," the first part of the sentence was sound, but the last part brought him under suspicion of tottering towards the marshy bog of sectarian mysticism.

The Disciples never taught the word-alone theory of conversion, but in some instances their conception of spiritual influence in turning men from darkness to light and from the power of Satan to God, resembled it so far that there was not much to choose between them. Men in this practical age would ask, What difference did it make so men were converted? And they would be right.

Mr. Campbell in his great debate with N.L. Rice in Lexington, Ky., in 1843, on the subject of spiritual influence, affirmed this proposition: "The Holy Spirit in conversion and sanctification operates only through the truth." The argument in support of this thesis is perhaps the most eloquent to be found in the literature of the Spirit's relation to saint and sinner, but it fails to carry conviction to the religious mind of today. Mr. Rice agreed with Mr. Campbell that the Spirit operated through the truth, but denied that it operated through the truth only. He said in his criticism of the adverb in the proposition, "If the Holy Spirit operates through the truth only, why does Mr. Campbell pray for the conversion of sinners?" Why not preach the Word, and leave the truth to do its work, without the invocation of an influence outside of both? If the affirmation is true, said the Presbyterian divine, that the spirit is shut up to the word of truth, the devil is more resourceful and powerful than God, for he reaches the minds of men without the intervention of words. Mr. Campbell did not answer these points, but the Disciples, for more than a generation, have answered them by the elimination of the word "only."

A child, today, in religious experience, and the study of Holy

Scripture, has learned some things about the divine Spirit not known to these giants of seventy years ago. Our people have been among the first to learn that the principal, though not the exclusive channel, of the Spirit's operation in conversion and sanctification, is the personality of regenerated and consecrated men and women. The circulation of the inspired word in heathen lands makes few if any converts, until word and Spirit find the opportunity of incarnation in the personality and holy character of the missionary, who carries to the dark lands of the earth the message of salvation. Peter's soul, illuminated by the Holy Spirit, and endued with power from on high, did more to convert the Pentecostians than the words of his sermon.

Otherwise a written communication, read by the people, would have done as well.

Our View on Fundamentals

In these latter days of up-to-dateness, the Disciples are in sympathy and touch with the best thought and deepest interpretation of the Holy Spirit and his offices in the work of redemption. They are in harmony with the best Christian scholarship in its findings on the present status of the Spirit question.

1. The Holy Spirit in the Old Testament is God in terms of life and energy. 2. It is the same in the New Testament up to John 14 where personal attributes are first ascribed to the Spirit. Where the Holy Spirit is referred to objectively the definite article is used; where it is referred to subjectively, the article is omitted, and it is simply "Holy Spirit." 3. On the day of Pentecost the Spirit appears as the element of a baptism administered by the risen and glorified Savior. This new spiritual baptism differentiates the Christian dispensation inaugurated by the Spirit's coming on Pentecost. 4. The gift of the Holy Spirit is promised to all true believers, the unction from the Holy One that brings the crowning and consciousness of sonship. Ye have an anointing or christening from the Holy One and

ye all know.

For a revival of interest and a restudy of the Spirit question, we are more indebted to J.H. Garrison and the *Christian-Evangelist*, and an illuminating book he wrote on the subject, than to any other human agency.

Have faith, repentance, and baptism been brought up to date among the Disciples? Do they need to move up in order to synchronize with the theological situation of the present day? We still preach "the old Jerusalem gospel" in its familiar triple conditions, but we put into them a greater depth and wealth of meaning than was done in the middle period of our history. There is always a tendency in an age of dispute and disruption to harden elements of the gospel into mental concepts and theorizing material, so mechanical and commercial as to be more interested in the salvation of definitions, plans and formulas, than in the salvation of souls. This was the old gospel of three steps into a house, three miles to a town, three sections to a bridge, more interested in conversion to a system of thought, apparently, than in the actual turning of the soul to God. We have passed almost entirely out of this period of a superficial intellectualism, and our only concern now is to emphasize these great gospel words and put into them the fullness and richness of meaning inspired by the Holy Spirit when it wrote the New Testament.

The searching inquiries of a century, and of many centuries from all sources, have confirmed and demonstrated our practice of immersion and believers' baptism, and the future is not likely to bring any change in this regard. In the matter of the design of baptism, or the relation of the ordinance to the remission of sins, or salvation, there has been a change, and an improvement. The dogmatic and legalistic construction of immersion as literally necessary to remission of sins, which arose out of the exigencies of controversy, and gave such mortal offense to our religious neighbors, unlike the voice of the turtle, in the Song of Songs, is not any more heard in the land.

We still believe that baptism is for the remission of sins, because the Bible says so, and so declare the historic creeds of Christendom; but that assertion throws us back on what the Bible and the creeds mean when they relate baptism to salvation. The church fathers used immersion and regeneration as interchangeable terms, because immersion was the symbol of regeneration. When Paul says the bath of regeneration saves us, he does not mean that the bath saved us, but it stood for the thing that did, regeneration. Water in religion signifies moral purification, the inward cleansing of the soul, and when the New Testament says that baptism is for the remission of sins, as a matter of course it puts the symbol for the thing symbolized, an allowable and very common form of speech.

While the Disciples will continue to practice immersion as the New Testament form of the ordinance that initiates and incorporates us into the body of Christ, they will spiritualize baptism very much as Paul spiritualized circumcision: "For a man who is only a Jew outwardly is not a real Jew; nor is outward bodily circumcision real circumcision. The real Jew is the man who is a Jew in soul; and the real circumcision is the circumcision of the heart, a spiritual and not a literal thing." (Rom. 2:28, 29.)

Baptism did not take the place of circumcision, but with Paul's consent, Disciple sanction, and permission of the translators of the twentieth century New Testament, the passage is thus brought up to date: "For a man who is only a Christian outwardly is not a real Christian; nor is outward bodily baptism real baptism. The real Christian is the man who is a Christian in soul; and the real baptism is the baptism of the heart, a spiritual and not a literal thing."

The Disciples have always been great on evangelism, and in these early decades of the twentieth century have become a leading factor in the educational and missionary forces of Christendom.

The Men and Millions Movement has no parallel in any other religious body. There has been no abatement or modification of the claim that as individuals we aim to be Christians or Disciples of

Christ, as congregations of believers, Churches of Christ; as a whole, collectively, a part of the church universal, and a movement within the church to bring back the lost unity of the apostolic church at the beginning.

The Work that Lies Before Us

The most timous and up-to-date document in the literature of our great union plea is the Declaration and Address by Thomas Campbell, that launched it a hundred years ago. The work that remains is to go forward to the New Testament and practical unification by way of the constitution of the Christian Association of Washington. Idealization of primitive Christianity and the ancient order of things would be harmless enough, provided its exploitation did not substitute a theoretical basis of union for the one foundation laid in Zion. Christendom will not unite on a human formulary. It is useless for men to draw one up. Evangelical churches are spiritually united in Christ and on Christ, and almost the only thing required to carry unity forward into union is the mutual recognition of each other as Christians and each other's churches as Churches of Christ, and practice in harmony with this action. This would tear down at a single stroke all separating walls, and the people of God would flow together into one great forward movement, to bring in the time when "They shall not teach every man his brother and every man his neighbor, saying, know the Lord, for all shall know him from the least to the greatest of them."

www.ingramcontent.com/pod-product-compliance
Lightning Source LLC
Chambersburg PA
CBHW061332040426
42444CB00011B/2877